THE WORK

OF ART

LONG LINES

FOREWORD BY DAVID QUAMMEN

Bozeman, Montana, is just a small town in the northern Rockies but it has its graces (if you don't mind the cold), it has its attractions (if you like mountains and trout), and consequently it's a place where some long lines cross. My own line happened to cross with Paul Bertelli's on an afternoon in the autumn of 1985, when we were both youngish, both new residents on a certain block in south Bozeman, and he happened to drop an old wood-frame storm window—he'd been trying to wrestle it into position—from three stories above a concrete driveway. Nobody got hurt, but what an announcement. Sixty feet away, I was minding my own business, probably cleaning gutters or raking leaves. I heard this godawful crash, looked across, looked up, saw a man in a high window with an Oops expression on his face, and became cheerily acquainted with my next-door neighbor. In the 29 years since, our friendship has grown and endured, and Paul has become considerably more expert about windows.

At that time, he was just six years into his work with Jonathan L. Foote. He had come out from Boston in 1972, a transfer student to Montana State University, and while studying architecture there, had become a sticker. A sticker is a person who knows just where he wants to make his life. I became a sticker in Montana also, though not foreseeing it at the time I arrived, one year later, in 1973. During the 1970s Paul and I paid our dues. Then in 1979, same year I quit my last job and took the leap as a freelance writer, he became Jonathan's first and only employee at the new firm, Jonathan L. Foote Architects. By 1985, when Paul and I met, JLF was going strong, and I too had begun to make a reasonable living from my chosen craft. Despite the fact that Paul was architectural and I was literary (more or less), we meshed. We got each other, and got what we were respectively trying to do.

What we were trying to do was in some ways the same thing: to make beautiful, lasting shapes by assembling elements from the real world, each piece selected for its inherent interest, its reliable heft and integrity, all put together into a unified whole. For me that meant word structures; for him it meant buildings. In each case our hope was that the whole, once assembled, would seem fresh, unexpected, even surprising, and at the same time inevitable

in its fitted grace. That he was creating elegant homes, in a neo-traditional Western vernacular, and that I was creating books and articles about science, in the vernacular of a writer heavily influenced by William Faulkner but with a taint of unseriousness that owed more to the Smothers Brothers, mattered less as a set of obvious differences than as a subtle coincidence of parallels. In the course of our friendship and very separate careers, as the small architectural firm became JLF Design Build, Paul understood these parallels better and sooner than I did. Not long ago, for instance, he said, David, you and I both know the terror of the blank page. I thought, thanks for reminding me.

Another obvious difference is that Paul works amid an intricately interactive team of partners and other collaborators, a group of talented people whose individual contributions—in ideas and drawings and plans, in steel and stone and wood, in glass and water and landscape itself—come together in the synergy that is a JLF project. Although I don't work entirely alone myself (I'm indebted to editors, sources, partners of various sorts), the orchestration of such a collective effort involves skills of leadership and diplomacy, and no doubt thrills of shared achievement, that I can only admire and envy from afar. In that role, Mr. Bertelli is more like a symphony conductor than like the grumpy, solitary writer who used to live next door.

The line that Paul and his partners Tammy, Logan, Ashley, John, and Jake have followed throughout their professional lives, the line that they have charted for JLF Design Build, is a long and graceful one reaching far beyond the south side of Bozeman, far beyond Montana, beyond even the Rocky Mountain West, in which its origin, inspiration, and aesthetic are anchored. But that line is not just a vector, an export route along which ideas, services, and deliverable projects have traveled outward to the wider world. The line doesn't just point; it connects. It's a path that leads back, for clients, for friends, for anyone who lays eyes on a JLF project, toward those things that are so wondrous and valuable about the particular place on America's map where it began.

THE WORK
OF ART

WRITTEN BY:
WILLIAM HJORTSBERG

PRINCIPAL PHOTOGRAPHER:
AUDREY HALL

ORO EDITIONS

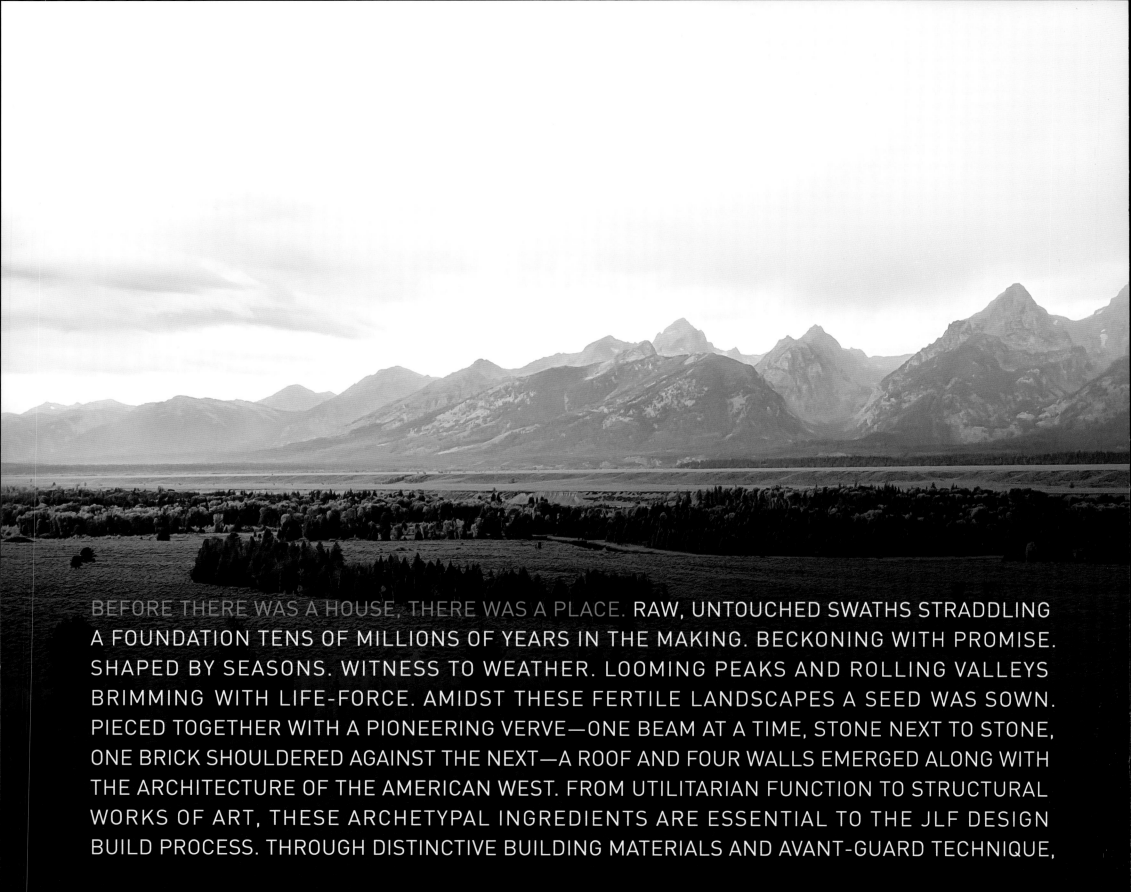

BEFORE THERE WAS A HOUSE, THERE WAS A PLACE. RAW, UNTOUCHED SWATHS STRADDLING A FOUNDATION TENS OF MILLIONS OF YEARS IN THE MAKING. BECKONING WITH PROMISE. SHAPED BY SEASONS. WITNESS TO WEATHER. LOOMING PEAKS AND ROLLING VALLEYS BRIMMING WITH LIFE-FORCE. AMIDST THESE FERTILE LANDSCAPES A SEED WAS SOWN. PIECED TOGETHER WITH A PIONEERING VERVE—ONE BEAM AT A TIME, STONE NEXT TO STONE, ONE BRICK SHOULDERED AGAINST THE NEXT—A ROOF AND FOUR WALLS EMERGED ALONG WITH THE ARCHITECTURE OF THE AMERICAN WEST. FROM UTILITARIAN FUNCTION TO STRUCTURAL WORKS OF ART, THESE ARCHETYPAL INGREDIENTS ARE ESSENTIAL TO THE JLF DESIGN BUILD PROCESS. THROUGH DISTINCTIVE BUILDING MATERIALS AND AVANT-GUARD TECHNIQUE,

AN AWARD-WINNING PERSPECTIVE WAS BORN. TODAY, WE ARE A COLLABORATION OF ARCHITECTS, ARTISANS, WOODWORKERS, STONEMASONS, BLACKSMITHS, CREATORS, DREAMERS, PHILOSOPHERS, AND PRAGMATISTS—DELIVERING MORE THAN THREE DECADES OF TIMELESS STRUCTURES ROOTED IN INTEGRITY AND SIMPLE ELEGANCE. WITH A FOOTPRINT THAT SPANS ROCKY MOUNTAIN LANDSCAPES TO BUCOLIC EXPANSES OF EASTERN BEARINGS, JLF DESIGN BUILD HAS CONTRIBUTED ITS MARK TO AN ANTHOLOGY OF ICONIC PLACE-BASED ARCHITECTURE. POWERED BY INSPIRED DESIGN AND AN EXACTING EYE FOR PLACEMENT, OUR ETHOS STEMS FROM A UNITY OF NATURE, BEAUTY, BALANCE, AND IMAGINATION. WELCOME TO THE WORK OF ART— A CONTINUUM OF A PROCESS THAT KNOWS NO LIMIT.

PUBLISHED BY
ORO EDITIONS
PUBLISHERS OF ARCHITECTURE, ART, AND DESIGN
GORDON GOFF: PUBLISHER
WWW.OROEDITIONS.COM
INFO@OROEDITIONS.COM

COPYRIGHT © 2014 BY ORO EDITIONS
ISBN: 978-1-941806-13-5
10 9 8 7 6 5 4 3 2 1 FIRST EDITION

CONCEPT AND DESIGN:
MAKE.
PORTLAND, MAINE
MAKE-STUDIO.COM

EDITED BY: RYAN BURESH
COLOR SEPARATIONS AND PRINTING: ORO GROUP LTD.
PRINTED IN CHINA.

THIS BOOK WAS PRINTED AND BOUND USING A VARIETY OF SUSTAINABLE MANUFACTURING PROCESSES AND MATERIALS, ACQUEOUS-BASED VARNISH, VOC- AND
FORMALDEHYDE-FREE GLUES, AND PHTHALATE-FREE LAMINATIONS. THE TEXT IS PRINTED USING OFFSET SHEETFED LITHOGRAPHIC PRINTING PROCESS IN FOUR COLOR ON
157GSM PREMIUM MATT ART PAPER WITH AN OFF-LINE GLOSS ACQUEOUS SPOT VARNISH APPLIED TO ALL PHOTOGRAPHS.

ORO EDITIONS MAKES A CONTINUOUS EFFORT TO MINIMIZE THE OVERALL CARBON FOOTPRINT OF ITS PUBLICATIONS. AS PART OF THIS GOAL, ORO EDITIONS, IN ASSOCIATION
WITH GLOBAL RELEAF, ARRANGES TO PLANT TREES TO REPLACE THOSE USED IN THE MANUFACTURING OF THE PAPER PRODUCED FOR ITS BOOKS. GLOBAL RELEAF IS
AN INTERNATIONAL CAMPAIGN RUN BY AMERICAN FORESTS, ONE OF THE WORLD'S OLDEST NONPROFIT CONSERVATION ORGANIZATIONS. GLOBAL RELEAF IS AMERICAN
FORESTS' EDUCATION AND ACTION PROGRAM THAT HELPS INDIVIDUALS, ORGANIZATIONS, AGENCIES, AND CORPORATIONS IMPROVE THE LOCAL AND GLOBAL ENVIRONMENT
BY PLANTING AND CARING FOR TREES.

LIBRARY OF CONGRESS DATA: AVAILABLE UPON REQUEST

FOR INFORMATION ON OUR DISTRIBUTION, PLEASE VISIT OUR WEBSITE
WWW.OROEDITIONS.COM

CONTENTS

THE STORY OF JLF DESIGN BUILD IS FAR RICHER AND MUCH MORE PROFOUND THAN ANYTHING A SIMPLE CHRONOLOGY CAN PROVIDE. ITS ESSENCE RUNS DEEPER THAN THE INDIVIDUAL HISTORIES OF ALL THOSE WHO TAKE PART IN THE PROCESS AND SHARE THE COMPANY'S CORE VALUES; TALENTED, DEDICATED PEOPLE, ALL OF WHOM OVER THE YEARS HAVE WORKED LONG AND HARD TO ACHIEVE THE IMPOSSIBLE – A NEVER-ENDING QUEST FOR PERFECTION. ART LIVES AT THE CENTER OF THIS NARRATIVE. THE CREATIVE SPIRIT PROVIDES ITS ESSENTIAL HEART AND SOUL.

To appreciate the eternal artistic impulse, imagine a journeyman stonemason in the 13th Century at work in an unfinished cathedral. The mason apprenticed in the same Master's workshop as had his father, who, more than three decades earlier, started working on the cathedral the year the foundation stones were set. Both were dead now, as the mason would be long before the completion of this glorious building. Many stones in the still-roofless cathedral bore the chiseled mark of the mason and his father.

By the time the grand edifice was finished almost a hundred years later, no one attending the consecration service knew who had made these marks. It was the mason's destiny to remain forever anonymous. A similar fate awaited the architect. The man who designed the beautiful Gothic building left no drawings or plans. Not even his name was recorded. All that survives 700 years later is the work. Man was born to build. The Luxor Temple survives along with the Parthenon and the magnificent ruined cities of the Roman Empire. There is true nobility in the dedicated, selfless endeavor required to create these splendid places.

The first guilds were organized in the Early Middle Ages. By 1400, craftsmen all across Europe formed guilds to promote their common interests. Four hundred years later, a secret fraternity adopted the mason's traditional tools as its symbols. The Founding Fathers became members.

This is interesting not for what it tells us about the past, but rather the questions it raises concerning the present. It's hard to imagine a time when things were made by hand, built by craftsmen who truly cared about their work. Where are the "guilds" of our time, the groups of artists and craftsmen today who combine their talents for a greater goal?

JLF Design Build shares that undying collective artistic spirit. At the company's core are ten talented individuals, some working together for almost three decades, who have provided continuity worthy of those medieval stonemasons. The history of the firm can be traced back to a log farmhouse on the banks of the Yellowstone River where in 1979 Paul Bertelli joined forces with Yale-trained architect, Jonathan L. Foote. The houses they designed were neo-traditional western buildings, subtle evocations of the past utilizing today's cutting-edge technology. The JLF aesthetic included salvaged 100-year-old, hand-hewn barn timbers, weathered siding, and recycled floorboards excoriated by a century of boot heels. Their houses looked authentic. They blended into the

Montana landscape as if they'd stood in the same spots for more than a century.

Early success encouraged growth and new talent signed on with JLF. Tammy Hauer was among the first. She joined the architectural firm in 1987 as their receptionist and bookkeeper. Over the next few years, her responsibilities increased and her position grew to Business Manager and CFO. "Incredibly proud" of her long experience with JLF Design Build, Tammy observes, "We as a firm have left a legacy in architecture that will live on forever."

In 1992, Logan Leachman became part of the JLF team. Over time, Logan discovered the firm's "sensitivity to design" dovetailed with his own "sensibilities." Building their own projects and "forming an informal design-build company" provided a new concept of "the collaborative way of doing the business of architecture." Over the years, Leachman climbed the ladder at JLF, becoming an integral part of the day to day management of the office.

Late in the 1990s, two architects with degrees from Montana State University joined the firm. John Lauman signed on first in 1997. It didn't take him long to realize that JLF was "highly specialized, almost singular" in its focus on elite, residential design-build. He cites the firm's "legacy of timeless western vernacular and harmony with the landscape" as the source of their continued success. Summing up his sixteen years at JLF Design Build, Lauman observes, "Clients know the difference between the innovators and the replicators. We always endeavor to far surpass the client's expectations."

When architect Jake Scott joined JLF in May of 1999, the concept of design-build was not all that common. "Most residences are built by a contractor," he says, looking back. "I didn't know about this niche." Over his years with the firm, Scott watched it evolve. The first projects he worked on were "very beautiful," but Jake states emphatically, "there is a difference between where we are now and how we were when I started." In that time, he learned the importance of getting to know the clients and learning to incorporate their personalities into the houses being designed for them. "Our projects wouldn't be what they are without the client's involvement," he says.

Upon Jon Foote's retirement in 2000, Jon sold the architecture firm to Paul Bertelli, Logan Leachman, Tammy Hauer, and Dick Storbo (retired) who became principals in the company.

"WHEN I THINK OF A JLF DESIGN BUILD PRODUCT, I FIRST THINK OF A STRUCTURE THAT WILL STAND THE TEST OF TIME. OUR BUILDINGS WILL STILL BE HERE IN 100 YEARS. WE'RE NOT MOTIVATED BY OUR COMPETITION BUT BY WHAT WE KNOW IS RIGHT. THAT, I THINK, IS WHAT GIVES US OUR SOUL."

John Lauman and Jake Scott stayed on, soon became associates, and recently became new partners. The JLF architect team is at present a tight-knit group of 21 and also includes Ashley, principal; associate Travis; project managers Shawn, Calbria, Terry, Tyler, and Ian; support technical staff Laurel, Matt, Stephanie, Andy, Kelsey, and Morgan; administrative staff Becky, Kim, and Sarah.

Jack Livingood met the JLF team after seeing photos of Paul's work in a couple magazines and hired them to design a house for him in Jackson, Wyoming. Jack is a third-generation builder from Salt Lake City. Jack's father, Dee Livingood, sold his blue VW bug in 1967 for $1,000 and used the money to start Big-D Construction, a company with a long design-build history in large commercial work. Now the CEO, Jack wanted Big-D to branch out into residential structures.

Livingood wanted top-notch people in his new Wyoming venture. Years of experience in the construction business taught him to look for men and women of the highest caliber. Scott Dansie grew up immersed in the building trades. After receiving his Bachelor's degree in Construction Management from Brigham Young University, Dansie spent over thirteen years as an estimator working for two large Utah contracting firms. During this time, he "gained a healthy respect for the capabilities and accomplishments of a key competitor." That company was Big-D Construction.

When he set out on his own as a consultant, Scott worked with Big-D Signature on several projects in the Jackson area. "Witnessing firsthand" their goal of wanting to be "the most sought after construction company in the business," his respect for the firm that had "a passion for trying to do things right in our industry," increased with every consulting job. In October of 2005, Livingood asked Dansie to join Big-D Signature full time as the Operations Officer for the Jackson office. Now President of Big-D Signature, he oversees residential construction in both the Jackson and Salt Lake City offices.

For Scott, this was "the opportunity to be part of the Process" and "contribute to the design and construction" of what he likes to call "interactive and reflective, timeless **art**itecture." Dansie puts the emphasis on Art, believing that JLF Design Build clients "don't just get a place to live, they really get a work of art. It reflects the character and personality and the desires of the individual owners and that begins from the very first meeting."

Born and raised in Jackson, Layne Thompson took architectural drafting for four years at high school. While studying Construction Management at BYU, Thompson began working during his senior year as an intern for Big-D Construction in Salt Lake City where he "had the opportunity to explore the design-build delivery method." After graduation in 2004, he moved back to Jackson and joined the Big-D Signature group. Over the next eight years, Layne worked as a Project Engineer, Estimator, Project Manager, Senior Estimator, and Preconstruction Manager, rising through the ranks to the position of Vice President with oversight of all Jackson-based projects.

"JLF Design Build is all about quality above all else," Thompson says. "When I think of a JLF Design Build product, I first think of a structure that will stand the test of time. Our buildings will still be here in 100 years. We're not motivated by our competition but by what we know is right. That, I think, is what gives us our soul."

Jason Dunlop was born in Salt Lake City and spent almost every childhood summer in Jackson, Wyoming. Jason studied computer science and graphic design at the University of Utah. By the time he left school, Dunlop was working part-time for a regional construction company. As a full-time employee, he worked his way up the ladder from "swinging a hammer to Project Manager." In 1997, Jason helped the company open an office in Jackson and here he first met Scott Dansie.

One day, Jason got a call from Scott Dansie, asking if he'd like to be the "business development guy" at Big-D Signature. Now Vice President, Jason handles not only business development, but field operations, human resources, and "anything else that comes across (his) desk."

With his healthy physique and close-cropped hair, Jason has the clean-cut appearance of a high school football coach. His gung-ho attitude brings an exuberant energy and "go for the goal" enthusiasm to his job. One employee once described the Process as "construction management nirvana." Dunlop knows this form of enlightenment. "You want that project to look like it's always been there."

Right from the start, there was something "organic" about this relationship that soon became "very dynamic and rich." Logan recalls that Jack "used his house as a training tank for his people to do residential projects. From the top down, he took all of his best people and rotated them through. Sometimes, you'd have a superintendent sweeping the floor. Some days, a project manager was running a saw. They all got hands-on experience."

The team at JLF also became a part of this process. "Everybody in this office would go on-site and learn from them," Leachman says. "And they would learn from us. We'd share knowledge about details. That was the start of our relationship." Jack felt proud of "decades honing our design-build skills." He and the JLF team "started talking about doing projects together." Their philosophies meshed perfectly. It was the beginning of a creative conversation still in progress.

In 2002, JLF Design Build moved into a 100-year-old building originally housing the Bozeman National Bank. That same year Ashley Sullivan, a Southern woman with a degree from Auburn University, joined the design-build team, becoming a partner in 2010. Her introduction to design-build was during her second year of architecture school. Ashley participated in the Rural Studio program that tasked the students to design and build a low cost housing project in Hale County, Alabama. Since then, she has confirmed that, "You can build quality design, make a space that is meaningful, that is site specific, and within budget." From Sullivan's first days

at JLF Design Build, she worked on major projects. She remembers learning the most "about myself and about design-build" from her work as Project Manager on a residence along the coast of Southern California. "I am proud of what I do," Ashley says, "and of the honesty that we all bring to the table. I want to give the clients their expectations in the best way possible."

The concept of design-build, where an architecture firm and a construction firm team up together, has been around for decades, but it took the collaboration between JLF and Big-D Signature to take this partnership to levels never before imagined. In nature, symbiosis is a term describing a mutually beneficial relationship between two different organisms. The word comes from the Greek and means "living together." The two entities become one.

The symbiotic partnership known as JLF Design Build has grown and enriched over the years to a place where, as Logan Leachman observes, "We're all on the same page 99% of the time." The core JLF Design Build team remains so in synch it's as if one person picks up a pencil and begins drawing a line and someone else takes over and continues the line and everyone agrees it's the same line. To describe their quest for perfection, a more accurate analogy might be an asymptote, a geometric concept where a curve approaches becoming a straight line, growing ever closer and closer as it reaches towards infinity. Absolute perfection remains an impossible goal, but day by day, hour by hour, JLF Design Build ventures as close as it can. It is the dedication that counts. ●

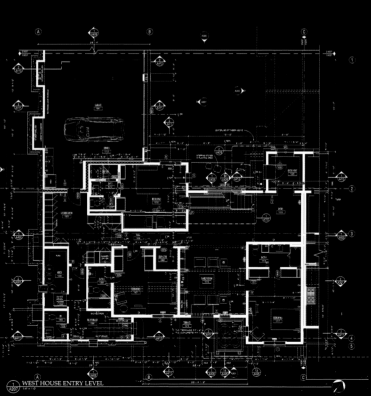

WEST HOUSE ENTRY LEVEL

① WEST ELEVATION
A5 ⅛" = 1'   0"

② NORTH ELEVATION
A5 ⅛" = 1'   0"

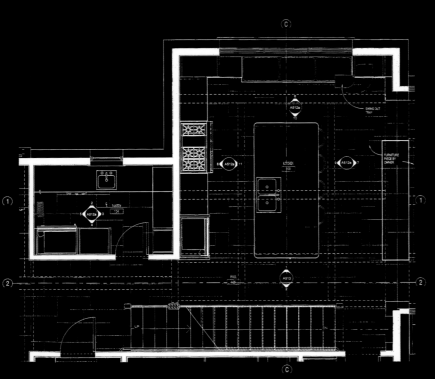

THROUGH THE RISING MIST OF LATE MORNING, THE HOUSE CALLED THE CREAMERY FLOATS LIKE AN APPARITION FAR OFF ABOVE A BROAD EXPANSE OF MEADOW AND POND. SERENE, ALMOST ETHEREAL, THE SIMPLE STONE BUILDING POSSESSES A TIMELESS QUALITY AS IF IT STOOD IN THIS LANDSCAPE FOR CENTURIES. FRAMED BY FIR TREES AGAINST THE MAJESTIC BACKDROP OF THE TOWERING TETON RANGE, THE CREAMERY IS ENHANCED, NOT DIMINISHED, BY ITS MAGNIFICENT SURROUNDINGS.

A first-time visitor to this splendid Wyoming house finds oneself pausing several times along the serpentine drive to admire the classic structure's simple elegance and to marvel at its dreamlike tranquility. Blink and it might be gone, a momentary intangible Brigadoon, come to life only once every hundred years. Knowing The Creamery's stone walls are two feet thick makes this storybook fantasy most remarkable. Built in the 1880s on the rolling plains about 15 miles south of Great Falls, Montana, by anonymous Scottish stonemasons whose names like those of the medieval cathedral builders have been swept away by the harsh winds of time. The old abandoned creamery sat roofless and deteriorating for almost half a century, just another lonely ruin, a silent monument to the skilled labor of long dead pioneers until its unexpected and glorious transformation. The story of The Creamery's resurrection has all the magic of a fairy tale.

When Bertelli learned of the abandoned creamery, he arranged for his client to travel up to the open field outside Great Falls and take a look. She was "emotionally overwhelmed" and decided on the spot to purchase the old building. It was disassembled in 2000, the stones drawn, numbered, and stacked on pallets.

In June of 2002, Paul made a perspective sketch of the house he and his client had been discussing. The ink drawing is loose in execution while remaining specific in detail. It looks remarkably like the finished structure. "Freehand sketches look more like the final house," Bertelli observed, "unlike the infinitely detailed and highly technical working drawings."

Throughout the design and construction of the house, the dialogue between the client and JLF continued as an open discussion. "It's a two-way street," she said, summing up her collaboration with the architects.

4 MAIN HOUSE/ CREAMERY - WEST ELEVATION

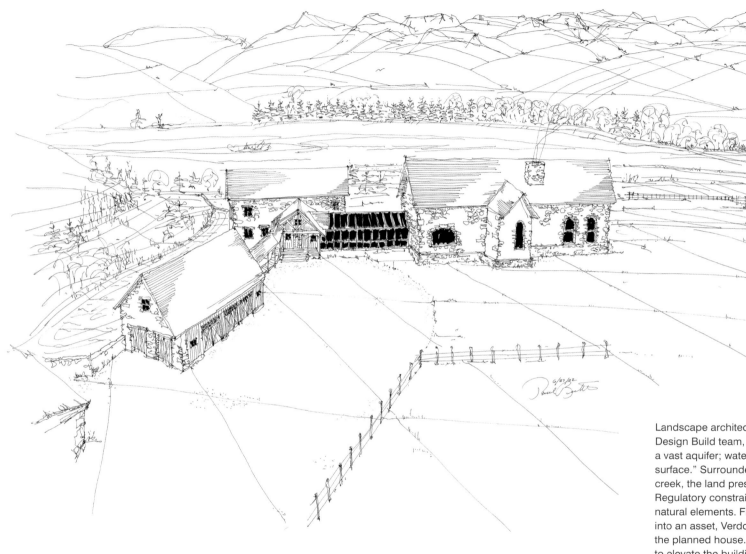

THAT WAS A SITUATION WHERE THE THREE LEGS OF THE STOOL CAME TOGETHER, THE CLIENT, THE ARCHITECT, AND THE LANDSCAPE ARCHITECT. – JIM VERDONE

Landscape architect, Jim Verdone, an integral part of the JLF Design Build team, recalls The Creamery property. "It sits on a vast aquifer; water that's only two, three, four feet below the surface." Surrounded by wetlands and containing a spring creek, the land presented potential issues for the builders. Regulatory constraints demanded setbacks from these fragile natural elements. Finding a way to turn an ecological liability into an asset, Verdone designed ponds in front and behind the planned house. The fill from these excavations was used to elevate the building site six feet above its original elevation to satisfy government regulations. Today, these ponds appear as if they'd existed since the dawn of time.

Having first seen the creamery "in its natural state," standing alone in an open field, the client wanted "the native grasses to flow right up against the front of the building." Verdone accommodated her desire not to have junipers or any shrubbery growing next to the house. The final result replicated the look of the old building as she remembered it, surrounded by meadowland and wild flowers, a noble survivor from a bygone age.

MAIN HOUSE/ CREAMERY - EAST ELEVATION
SCALE 1/8"=1'-0"

1 MAIN HOUSE - NORTH ELEVATION
A20 A3.0 SCALE: 1/8"=1'-0"

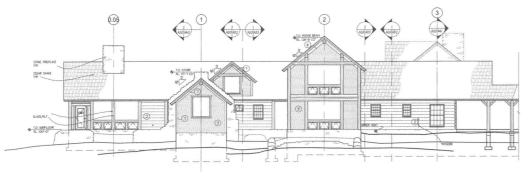

3 MAIN HOUSE/ CREAMERY - SOUTH ELEVATION
A20 A3.0 SCALE: 1/8"=1'-0"

THE JLF DESIGN BUILD CREW IS "SO GOOD AT MAKING THEIR BUILDINGS LOOK LIKE THEY'VE BEEN THERE FOREVER."

To this day, Layne, who worked as the project engineer on The Creamery, considers it the favorite of all his projects. It "has a soul and spirit of its own," he says, representing "the pinnacle of collaboration with a very engaged client and an architect/builder team." Logan believes that "the dedication to pull that off ripples all the way down to what happens at the foundation; those team members working on structural details and rebar." At the end of the process, the JLF Design Build team created a magical space, one replicating the tranquility of medieval chapels. "You walk in and you're at peace," Paul observed.

The JLF Design Build crew is "so good at making their buildings look like they've been there forever," Jim observed. "What we build are brand-new hundred year old houses," says Jason. Jack agrees, calling The Creamery "a stunning house." While it remains his favorite of all Bertelli's designs, Jack is quick to add, "I honestly believe Paul is doing the best work of his career right now." •

WHEN THE FOLKS AT JLF DESIGN BUILD TALK ABOUT WHAT MAKES THEIR WORK SO EXTRAORDINARY, THEY ALL PAY HOMAGE TO "THE PROCESS." AFTER MORE THAN THIRTY YEARS SPENT PERFECTING THE PROCESS, IT IS "EMBEDDED IN OUR CULTURE AND OUR CORE VALUES." TOGETHER, JLF AND BIG-D ARE "A COMPANY ON A MISSION, AND RELENTLESSLY IN MOTION." ACCORDING TO JACK, "OUR PROCESS IS A HUMAN ONE. IT'S MORE ABOUT CULTURE, PHILOSOPHY, AND A LOT OF HUMAN BEINGS FIGURING OUT HOW TO WORK TOGETHER THAN IT IS ABOUT ANY PARTICULAR FORMULA FOR EVERY HOUSE." FOR PAUL, IT'S NOT A PRODUCT, IT'S A PROCESS.

"THE JOY IS IN THE PURSUIT. IT DRIVES EVERYTHING!"

SEE DETAILED JLF DESIGN BUILD PROCESS ON PAGE 234

The best way to understand the inner-workings of their process is to track a client from the moment he, she, or they first decide to buy a piece of property and build a house on it. Not just any house. Something special designed by a distinguished architect. Finding the most suitable architect isn't quite the same thing as hiring the right plumber. Even with the majority of JLF's new work coming from client referrals, the highest of all accolades, the firm still has to compete on the marketplace. In the course of exploring Jackson Hole, one couple from New Jersey came across several JLF Design Build houses. "We ended up gravitating toward houses by this particular architect," they recalled. Particularly impressed by a number of buildings at Shooting Star, the couple knew at that moment who should design their house. "A good architect really does stand out," they said. JLF Design Build designed the Shooting Star cabins, a complex of eighteen houses. The cabins "really knocked our socks off," the couple recalled. JLF got the job in a "walkaway."

Often, at the beginning of the Process, JLF Design Build assists a new client in finding the right piece of property. Locating the correct building site on the chosen property is very important. Before the actual design work begins, the house must sit in its proper place within the landscape and meet the client's expectations. Selecting that site is critical to Paul. "This is the canvas," he observes.

"Art as architecture isn't a static element," Verdone says. "It is something that evolves throughout the whole project."

Planning and Programming, the first stage of the Process, is by necessity the most intimate moment in the client-designer relationship. "Our process is very intensive at the programming stage," Leachman notes. "We want to know what is important to you (the client)." Throughout long conversations with the architects, the New Jersey couple made it clear they wanted "a house that was right for Wyoming," one expressing "the Western vernacular." They had no interest in building "a faux house," some overblown stage set out of Bonanza. "The use of glass and all that leaves no doubt to the observer that this is a modern house," the client said, "not a restoration."

Each stage in the Process generates its own budget. Because the cornerstone of JLF Design Build's core philosophy is to keep the owner in control of his project, each individual budget must be client approved before moving on to the next stage. The Planning and Programming budget is speculative by its very nature. At this point, nothing yet is drawn on paper. "The project is just square footage areas," according to Big-D Signature estimator, Greg Casperson. It is a conversation with the client about numbers and size. How many rooms in all? How many bathrooms? Showers, tubs or both? Number of fireplaces? Lighting control system? The architect encourages his client. These discussions can last six hours or more. "No stone is left unturned," Bertelli says. "It's their house. It's not our house."

The intensity of these initial meetings reflects JLF Design Build's belief in "always telling the truth to a client even at the risk of losing the job." They feed their clients so much information up front in order to control the risk right from the start. These can be houses with big price tags and JLF wants the client to understand how the Process works from day one. "Why are we doing it?" is most often the first question asked. In order to succeed, the Process demands complete honesty at every stage, especially during the initial steps when everything is about concept and no serious expenses have accrued. If the costs look too high, project details can be modified, square footage reduced. "You never build a house twice," Paul says. "You've only got one shot."

IN ORDER TO SUCCEED, THE PROCESS DEMANDS COMPLETE HONESTY AT EVERY STAGE.

ALWAYS TELL THE TRUTH, EVEN AT THE RISK OF LOSING THE JOB.

Out of notes generated from these first discussions, JLF Design Build prepares budgets for the client based on alternate programs and their projected square footage. Preliminary costs for the differing programs are established, along with hardscaping (patios, outdoor dining, terracing), outbuildings (shed, gazebos, pergolas), and infrastructure (septic system, road, water lines, electric power, "all the stuff that goes in the ground;" things you often cannot see). Budgets are presented to the client for selection and approval, starting with an Executive Summary. This presentation procedure will remain the same until the end of the project.

At the beginning of Concept Diagrams, the second stage in the Process, JLF Design Build develops several bubble diagrams, simple amorphous shapes locating the house and any outbuildings in relation to the landscape. These are meant as concepts, a shorthand form of solving the big picture. "It's all about the relationship with the land and the scenery," one client observed. At this stage, the budgets are based on square foot costs, historical data, market conditions, and site complexity; they are not yet quantity cost estimates of an actual building.

The Schematic Design phase is the essence of the design, expressing the character of the building, materials, and massing. Hand drawn sketches, plans, and elevations provide another opportunity for the client to share in the Process. Also, a second budget takes a new look at the project, providing updated cost estimates – now quantity cost estimates based on the actual design drawings of the building. "We take that new estimate and we compare it back to the numbers from the planning and programming estimate," Greg Casperson explains. Transparency is critical. "We always give a comparison and when something has changed significantly (up or down) in terms of scope, it is tracked via an audit trail." Once the owner approves these schematic designs and the new resulting budget, the project moves to Design Development.

During Design Development, schematic design drawings, floor plans, and elevations are converted to AutoCAD and Revit. They are metamorphosed into working documents. By this stage, consultants (mechanical, electrical, and structural engineers) have been hired. Their input is vital. The consultants supply the project estimator with information required for the DD budget. These individual budgets allow clients separate opportunities to weigh in on cost control and design elements. Many complex details have to be digested, methodically timed, and coordinated with the construction schedule.

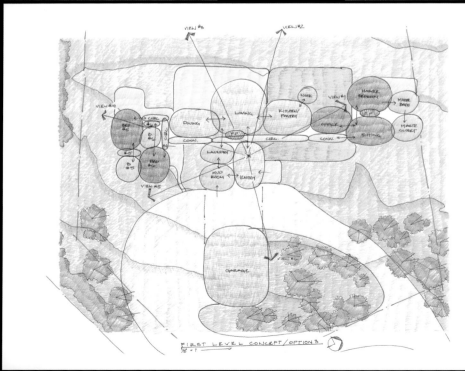

PLANNING AND PROGRAMMING, THE FIRST STAGE OF THE PROCESS, IS BY NECESSITY THE MOST INTIMATE MOMENT IN THE CLIENT-DESIGNER RELATIONSHIP.

As part of the process, JLF Design Build holds regular conferences to discuss the developing project. These meetings are usually conducted on a weekly basis. The clients are encouraged to participate. Both companies have their conference rooms fitted out with video conference systems. The participants sit in separate offices in Montana and Wyoming, talking freely as if gathered in the same room. "We really have to communicate a lot in the beginning of these projects," Jack says. "We would wear our tires out getting to Bozeman and they would wear their tires out coming down here. These collaborative meetings and the screens are really just an overflow of how can we do this better."

Once the DD budget has been approved by the client, JLF Design Build finalizes the construction documents and develops the Control Estimate, a critical segment of the Process. Construction bid sets (a collection of plans specific to each designated task) are now prepared. These bid sets, various schedules, specifications, and the drawings are used to prepare the Control Estimate. At the same time, plan sets are prepared for municipality officials (building and fire departments, planning, zoning) for review, a process that can take between five and eight weeks until a final building permit is issued. This varies wildly from one jurisdiction to another. Also, the project estimator goes over the plans to "poke holes in the bidability." He needs to be certain there's enough information so everyone is on the same page when the bids come in, final choices made, and contracts written. The goal is to identify "scope gap" early enough to avoid unexpected problems further down the line, saving the client from unplanned expenses.

074

THE GOAL IS TO IDENTIFY "SCOPE GAP"
EARLY ENOUGH TO AVOID UNEXPECTED
PROBLEMS FURTHER DOWN THE LINE.

A typical weekly conference during this stage of the Process provides an inside look at the thousands of other similar meetings JLF Design Build has conducted. Ashley sits at the JLF table with Tyler Call, the JLF project manager. Images of pages from the construction plans are captured by ceiling-mounted cameras and fill the two big Sony flat screens on the northern wall of the conference room. Smaller inserts show the project site supervisor, the project manager, and the project engineer gathered for the meeting down in Jackson. The client is on speakerphone, an active participant in the discussion.

Strict attention to the smallest detail keeps the Process on track. No item is deemed too small. The philosophical heart of everything JLF Design Build believes in means including the client's input at every stage. This owner sits in by phone at all scheduled meetings, asking pointed, intelligent questions, making certain her finished house is the home she envisioned all along. Clearly pleased with the detailed answers to her many queries, she says, "I'm properly humbled," at the end of the session before hanging up until next week.

JLF Design Build maintains an open book accounting proc
opportunity to examine the data whenever they choose. "S
line items," says Chandra Weston, the job cost accounta
"They don't necessarily want to see the invoice that backs th
clients who actually want to see that invoice. It just varies de
comfort." Tammy concurs. "If a client requests any individu
records, anything detailed, that's all available to them."

After a series of meetings, document reviews, and revised d
are reviewed with the client and a final selection of the su
At this point, the Control Estimate budget is prepared. It co
project's estimated cost. To help inform the client when to m
the remaining design items, the design team engages in ove
"There is nothing more cost effective than putting the perf
exactly the right time."

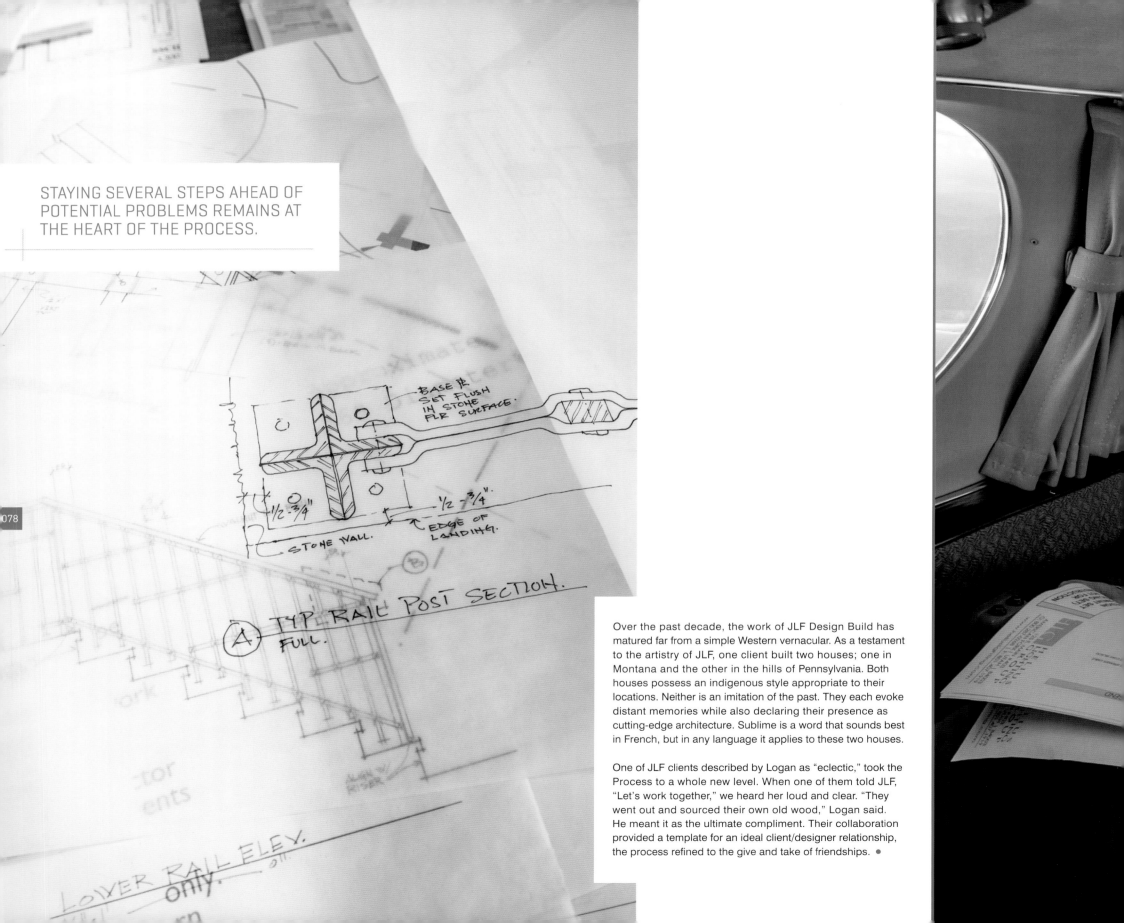

STAYING SEVERAL STEPS AHEAD OF
POTENTIAL PROBLEMS REMAINS AT
THE HEART OF THE PROCESS.

BASE ℞
SET FLUSH
IN STONE
FLR SURFACE.

½-¾"

½-¾"

STONE WALL.

EDGE OF
LANDING.

B

A TYP. RAIL POST SECTION.
FULL.

LOWER RAIL ELEV.
only.

Over the past decade, the work of JLF Design Build has
matured far from a simple Western vernacular. As a testament
to the artistry of JLF, one client built two houses; one in
Montana and the other in the hills of Pennsylvania. Both
houses possess an indigenous style appropriate to their
locations. Neither is an imitation of the past. They each evoke
distant memories while also declaring their presence as
cutting-edge architecture. Sublime is a word that sounds best
in French, but in any language it applies to these two houses.

One of JLF clients described by Logan as "eclectic," took the
Process to a whole new level. When one of them told JLF,
"Let's work together," we heard her loud and clear. "They
went out and sourced their own old wood," Logan said.
He meant it as the ultimate compliment. Their collaboration
provided a template for an ideal client/designer relationship,
the process refined to the give and take of friendships. ●

083

SIMMS

One of JLF Design Build's few commercial projects serves as a prime example of just how far from any cubbyhole the firm's vision has taken them. Paul first met the CEO of Simms on a fly fishing trip to Chile and for a number of years afterwards they "spent a fair amount of time on the water together." Simms manufactures fishing apparel and is the only company still making waders in America. When the firm relocated to the Four Corner's area just west of Bozeman, Montana, it purchased a large, sterile, uninspired industrial building, the former business of a retail hardware center.

The immediate problem facing Simms in their new headquarters was space. While in concept, this newer building had plenty of room for Simms's manufacturing end, there wasn't enough office space. The first architect the CEO consulted suggested "just bolting 10,000 square feet on the end of the beige building." The businessman felt there had to be a better solution and gave his old fishing buddy a call.
Paul took a look at the drab industrial structure and knew this was not the way Simms wanted to advertise its brand. "This is an opportunity to really reinvent how you present Simms to the public," Paul told his potential client.

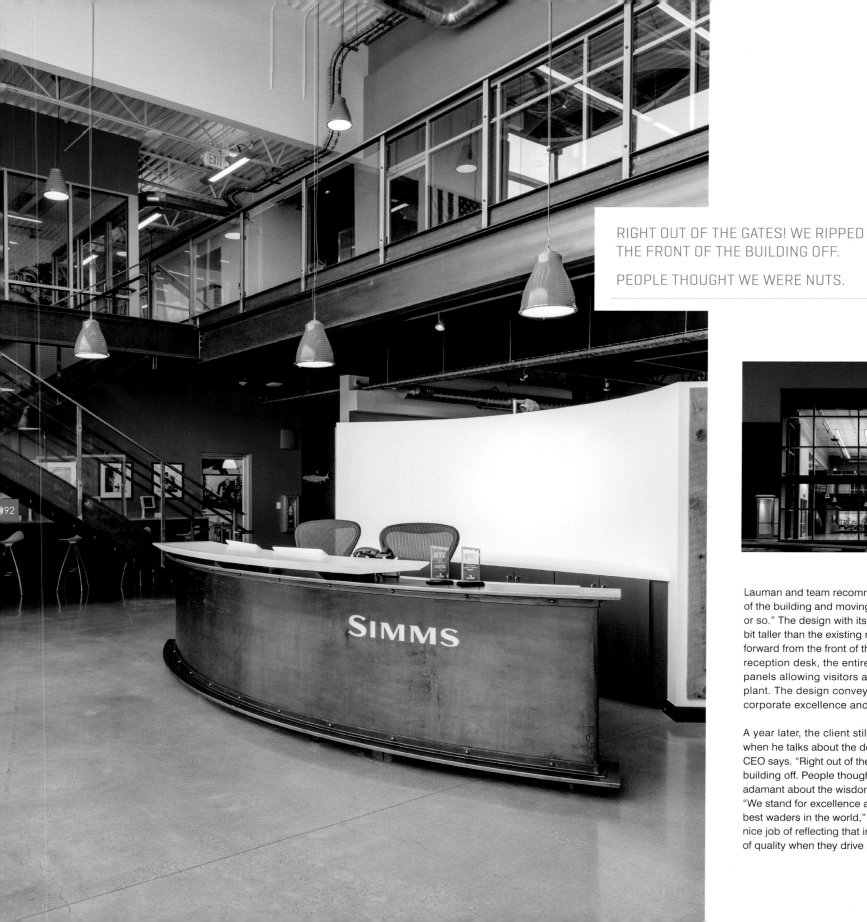

RIGHT OUT OF THE GATES! WE RIPPED
THE FRONT OF THE BUILDING OFF.

PEOPLE THOUGHT WE WERE NUTS.

Lauman and team recommended tearing off the entire front of the building and moving the facade out by "fifteen feet or so." The design with its two-story glass cube lobby is a bit taller than the existing roofline and thrusts dramatically forward from the front of the building. Inside, behind the reception desk, the entire back wall is made up of glass panels allowing visitors a look into the manufacturing plant. The design conveys a powerful concept of corporate excellence and transparency.

A year later, the client still expresses a sense of wonder when he talks about the design. "He nailed it," the Simms CEO says. "Right out of the gates! We ripped the front of the building off. People thought we were nuts." The CEO remains adamant about the wisdom of taking this radical direction. "We stand for excellence and pride ourselves on making the best waders in the world," he explains. "JLF has done a really nice job of reflecting that in the building. People get a sense of quality when they drive up."

BEFORE LINES ON MAPS. IN A BORDERLESS COUNTRY, PRIMAL AND ALL GUTS. PRECEDING RENAISSANCE, REVOLUTION, POST-MODERNISM, SPACE DETONATION, SUBURBAN SPRAWL, AND ENVIRONMENTAL CALL-TO-ARMS. RIVERS, LAKES, AND OCEANS WERE FIRST. TODAY THEY ARE ELIXIRS INDICATIVE OF HEALTH. THE MORE TIME IMMERSED, THE BETTER WE FEEL. THE MORE SPENT ADRIFT ELSEWHERE, THE DEEPER WE ACHE TO RETURN. IT'S OUR ADDICTION. IT'S RELIGION. AND IT'S PHILOSOPHY, ECONOMICS, AND ART ALL SMASHED INTO ONE. IT'S NOTHING BUT IONS, MOLECULES, AND PARTICLES. AND YET IT IS EVERYTHING. AT SIMMS THESE AQUEOUS ENVIRONMENTS ARE OUR ROOT. AND IN BOZEMAN, MONTANA, WITHIN THIS STATE-OF-THE-ART 62,000 SQUARE-FOOT FACILITY, THEY REPRESENT OUR FUTURE. THROUGH FOUR SEASONS WE FLOW TO THE TUNE OF SKILLED TECHNICIANS—TRAINED HANDS AND FISH-HONED MINDS THAT STITCH SOUL AND INSPIRATION INTO EVERY USA-MADE WADER THAT MARCHES INTO THE CURRENT. THIS IS WHERE WE LIVE TO FISH. AND FISH TO LIVE. A PLACE WHERE FIELD-TESTING AND R&D IS A BACKYARD OF UNRELENTING OUTSIDE OPPORTUNITY. AND WHERE ENGINEERING, DESIGN, AND FABRIC ARCHITECTURE WORK IN HARMONY TO WAGE WAR AGAINST THE ELEMENTS. WELCOME TO SIMMS. BUILT FOR TODAY. POWERED BY ON-THE-WATER INNOVATION FOR TOMORROW.

AUTHENTIC

FISHING GEAR

BOZEMAN · MONTANA

WADERS   FOOTWEAR   OUTERWEAR   LAYERING   WOMEN'S   SPORTSWEAR   VESTS + PACKS + BAGS

Maine-based advertising and design firm Make, contributed to the bold dramatic look of the Simms headquarters. Dan Bryant, founder at Make, "rendered the exterior paint job," incorporating gray and black with a Simm's signature orange horizontal band running the length of the facade. "Dan is also responsible for the branding and graphic presentations in the building," the CEO said. These include a huge black and white photomural of a saltwater flats guide filling the lobby's entire northern wall. Dan praises the CEO's unrelenting vision in pursuit of excellent design for the Simms headquarters.

Dan had directed and produced a short black-and-white documentary-style film that celebrated Simms without ever mentioning the company by name. Set in a remote Alaskan fly fishing camp, the film portrays fishing guides and their clients all wearing Simms gear. It's a subtle and inspired promotional work. Paul loved Dan's film, "It spoke volumes about that culture with very few words." "Dan and Paul both have a keen aesthetic sense and they work really well together," the Simms CEO observed. ●

CHICAGO METALLIC
CURVGRID - 381.60.10

CHICAGO METALLIC
CURVGRID - 332.60.10

CHICAGO METALLIC
CURVGRID - 381.45.06

CHICAGO METALLIC
CURVGRID - 382.45.06

CHICAGO METALLIC
CURVGRID - 381.60.10

CHICAGO METALLIC
CURVGRID - 382.60.10

3FORM FISH LET IN TO BUTT
JOINT OLD WOOD WITH
PERIMETER LED STRIPS

EAST ELEV
AX.X A3.0   SCALE 1/8"

TOP OF ROOF

32'-6 1/4"

A GREAT COMPOSER MIGHT BE A GENIUS, BUT LACKING AN ORCHESTRA,
THERE IS NO SYMPHONY.

ENLARGED SILO PLAN LEVEL #2

2
A529

SILO LANDINGS

4
A529

ONLY A FEW OF THE HUNDREDS OF CRAFTSMEN AND ARTISANS THAT WORK ON OUR PROJECTS ARE FEATURED IN THIS BOOK. IT IS HERE THAT WE FAITHFULLY TRY TO HONOR ALL THOSE WHO CONTRIBUTED THEIR TALENTS TO OUR WORK. FORGIVE US IF WE MISSED A FEW.

1-LEVEL	BILL KOLP	COAST CONCRETE & MASONRY	GREG CASPERSON
3-D FIRE PROTECTION	BIOTA RESEARCH	COAST SHEET METAL, INC.	GUNNISON PLUMBING AND MECHANICAL
3FORM	BIOSEAL	COASTAL ROOFING COMPANY	HALLIN & ASSOCIATES
A+ ELEVATORS & LIFTS	BLACK BOX DESIGN	COMFORT SYSTEMS OF MONTANA, INC.	HARKER DESIGN
ACCESS CONSULTING, PC	BLACK IRON DESIGN, INC.	CONCEPT STUDIO	HAYNES-ROBERTS, INC.
ACW CONSTRUCTION	BOB KNORI	CORE STONEWORKS	HEART FOUR IRONWORKS
ADAPTIVE DESIGN GROUP, INC.	BRADY CRAWFORD	CROWN CREATIONS	HEATHER MADDEN DESIGN
ADVANCED CONCRETE SOLUTIONS	BRENT NELSON	CURT CANNON	HERSHBERGER DESIGN
ADVANCED CUSTOM ELECTRIC	BRENT PARK	CUSTOM WINDOWS	HIGH PLAINS DRILLING
AEGIS ENGINEERING, INC.	BRESSLER INSULATION, INC.	D.P. LUND COMPANY	HILARY HEMINWAY INTERIORS
ALADDIN INDUSTRIES, INC.	BRETT VOORHEES	DALE BLACKETT	HOPE'S WINDOWS, INC.
ALAN GADBERRY	BRIAN ALLEN	DALE TURNER	HOPPE BROTHERS AND SONS
ALESSANDRA BRANCA	BRIAN'S HARDWOOD FLOORS, INC.	DARIAN MCGAVIN	HUNT ELECTRIC, INC.
ALEX THIERAULT	BRIDGER ENGINEERS, INC.	DAVE HUTCHISON	HYALITE ENGINEERS, PLLC
ALICIA AIR CONDITIONING & HEATING	BRIDGER KITCHENS	DEPENDABLE PAINT	I.C. THOMASSON ASSOCIATES, INC.
ALLEN'S GARAGE DOORS	BRIDGER TILE & STONE	DILBECK BROTHERS MASONRY	IDS ELECTRICAL ENGINEERS, INC.
ALLIED ENGINEERING SERVICES, INC.	BROMBAL USA	DJON WILSON	IN CONCRETE
ALPINE SURVEYING, INC.	BUCKHORN GEOTECH, INC.	DONAHUE MCNAMARA STEEL, LLC	INDEPENDENT POWER SYSTEMS
AMEC EARTH & ENVIRONMENTAL, INC.	C&H ENGINEERING AND SURVEYING	DOOR TECH, INC.	INDUSTRIAL CONTRACTORS, INC.
ANATRA CABINETRY	C&W EXCAVATION	DUNN ASSOCIATES, INC.	INTERIOR ENVIRONMENTS, INC.
APEX ENGINEERING SERVICES, INC.	CAPSTONE CONSTRUCTION	DW TILE & NATURAL STONE	INTERMOUNTAIN AQUATICS, INC.
APLIN MASONRY	CARL MCCAY	EJ INTERIOR DESIGN	INTERMOUNTAIN ROOFING, INC.
ARCHITECTURAL STONE & TILE	CARSON CONCRETE	ERON JOHNSON ANTIQUES	JACK FULLER
ARNELL KASE	CASHMAN NURSERY & LANDSCAPING	EUROPEAN MARBLE & GRANITE	JACKSON PAINT & GLASS
ARTISAN DOORS	CATHERINE LANE INTERIORS	FATES FLOORING	JAMES GUTKE
ASSOCIATES III INTERIOR DESIGN	CDP ENGINEERS, INC.	FEDERATION ANTIQUES, INC.	JANE SCHWAB AND CINDY SMITH
B.K. [IN MEMORY]	CERI CHAPPLE	FENESTRATION PARTNERS, INC.	JB MECHANICAL
BACKWOODS DESIGN	CHAMPION PAINTING, INC.	FERNANDO MARTINEZ	JENNIFER SPRENGLER
BAIN CAMPBELL	CHANDRA WESTON	FEUZ EXCAVATION	JEREMY MERRILL
BAR MILL IRON FORGE	CHINKER CHICKS	FISH CREEK EXCAVATION	JERRED STRADLEY
BARE'S STOVE & SPA, INC.	CHINO STEEL	FISHER MARANTZ STONE	JGM GROUP, LLC
BART WEGHORST	CHRISTA GERTISER	FOLEY ASSOCIATES, INC.	JIM CAMOU
BASSETT PAINTING	CHUCK'S GLASS	FORTENBERRY CONSTRUCTION	JIM FIFLES
BAUER & ASSOCIATES	CHURCH & ASSOCIATES	FOUR CORNERS CONCRETE	JIM HARMON
BEN DANIEL	CLAIR SHARP	FRED LOWERY	JIM IPEKJIAN
BEN PAGE & ASSOCIATES	CLAY TURNER	GARY DANSIE	JM ENGINEERING, PLLC
BIG ASS FANS	CLAYTON TROEGLE	GEOSOLUTIONS INTERNATIONAL	JOE URBANI & ASSOCIATES
BIG SKY MASONRY	CLOE ERICKSON	GPD, PC	JOHN DANBY
BIG SKY WATERPROOFING	CN ENGINEERS	GREEN STRUCTURAL ENGINEERING, INC.	JON EATON

JORGENSEN ASSOCIATES, PC
JOSE FERRER
JPI ENGINEERING, PC
JUDD MILLER
JULIE BUDAY-WILLIS
JULIE HAMILTON
JUST STONE
JWC CONSULTING ENGINEERS, PLLC
KATIE DAHLGREN
KAYLYNE ANDERSON
KEITH MCCOY
KENNY RASMUSSEN
KENYON NOBLE
KERRY WELCH
KRISTIANSEN ASSOCIATES
LAKE GLASS
LARA CILO
LAURA WHITE
LEE COMPANY
LINDA IVERSON DESIGN & MAINTENANCE
MACKENZIE MASONRY
MAJA LISA ENGELHARDT
MAKE
MARCUS ALBITRE
MARKHAM ROBERTS, INC.
MARSTON AND LANGINGER
MAVERICK CREATIONS
MAXIMO VINCENTE-SARAT
MAYVILLE LANDSCAPING
MD NURSERY AND LANDSCAPING, INC.
MECHCO, INC.
MIDWEST STEEL INDUSTRIES, INC.
MIGUEL GARCIA
MIKE MAYER
MIKE WINTERS
MIKE'S HEATING
MITCHELL HARDWOOD FLOORING
MODERN LIGHTING & ELECTRIC
MOLARO USA

MONTANA EXPRESSIONS
MONTANA PONDS, INC.
MONTANA READY MIX
MONTANA RECLAIMED LUMBER
MONTANA SASH & DOOR
MONTANA TILE & STONE
MORRISON-MAIERLE, INC.
MOUNTAIN HIGH WOODWORKS
MOUNTAIN LAND DESIGN, INC.
MOUNTAIN WEST HEATING & AIR CONDITIONING
NANAWALL
NELSON ENGINEERING
NIELSON ENGINEERING, INC.
NISHKIAN MONKS, PLLC
NORTHERN ROOF TILES
OLD FAITHFUL FIRE SPRINKLERS
OLE OLESEN
ON SIGHT LAND SURVEYORS, INC.
ON SITE MANAGEMENT
OPTIMUM WINDOW
OWEN CONSTRUCTION
PALEY STUDIOS, LTD.
PAUL CLEMENTI
PCH ELECTRIC
PEAK GLASS
PERMAFLOORS
PETER BRANDES
PETERSEN MASONRY
PHANTASTIC PHAUX
PHOENIX FIRE PROTECTION
PIERSON LAND WORKS, LLC
PIONEER LOG SYSTEMS, INC.
POINDEXTER'S
POND AND STREAM CONSULTING, INC.
QUARRY WORKS
R. HIGGINS DESIGN
RANGER PLUMBING
REILLY'S DRYWALL
RENDEZVOUS ENGINEERING, PC

RESNET KWA
RICHARD KEITH LANGHAM
ROBERT BUMP CONSTRUCTION
ROBIN B. HAMERS & ASSOCIATES
ROCKY MOUNTAIN STEEL, INC.
ROWENA FINEGAN
RYAN BIRCH
RYAN HARMON
RYDALCH ELECTRIC, INC.
SALT RIVER ROOFING
SAM STEVENS
SANDVOL MASONRY
SCOTT BREWER
SCOTT'S WELDING AND MACHINE SHOP
SEATON EARTHMOVERS, INC.
SELECT STONE, INC.
SHANDON BRINKERHOFF
SHAWN TERRY
SHEET METAL SPECIALTIES
SIMKINS-HALLIN, INC.
SKIDMORE, INC.
SMART STEEL
SOMMERS PLASTER
SPIRAL STAIRS OF AMERICA
SPRINKLER TECHNOLOGY DESIGN, INC.
STANDARD DRYWALL
STEEL WEST, INC.
STEVE HILL
STILEWOOD INTERNATIONAL
STONE SOURCE
STONEWORKS OF JACKSON HOLE
STUDIO AV
T&G FLOORING
TATE HOYLE
TAYLOR EASTIN
TAYLOE PIGGOTT
TDG WORKS, INC.
TECH ELECTRIC
TERI SOKOLEK

TERRI EVENSON
TERRY EARL
THOMAS MURPHY
THOMPSON POOLS
TLM INTERIOR DESIGNERS
TONKS MASONRY
TOTAL ELECTRIC OF MONTANA
TRAIL CREEK NURSERY
TYLER COOPER
TYLER DUNN
UBALDO VINCENTE
VALLEY FRAMING, INC.
VALLEY GLASS
VEERE GRENNEY ASSOCIATES
VERN CAMPBELL
VLA, INC. (VERDONE LANDSCAPE ARCHITECTS)
WATCHGUARD SECURITY SYSTEMS
WATER WERKS, INC.
WAYNE COOPER
WEBER DRILLING
WEBER PLUMBING
WEST POINTE ELECTRIC, INC.
WESTWOOD CURTIS CONSTRUCTION, INC.
WILD WEST IRON WORKS, INC. (SCOTT ESPELIN)
WILLIAMS PLUMBING & HEATING
WILLOW CREEK WOODWORKS, INC.
WILSON CABINETRY
WOMACK & ASSOCIATES, INC.
WRJ DESIGN ASSOCIATES
WYNN BIRCH
WYOMING DRYWALL
WYOMING GLASS WORKS
WYOMING LANDSCAPE CONTRACTORS, INC.
WYOMING MECHANICAL CO., INC.
WYOMING WOOD FLOORS
YELLOW IRON EXCAVATING, LLC
ZACHARY MCDERMOTT

CO-DESIGNED BY PAUL BERTELLI & W.K. WEISSMAN

CO-DESIGNED BY PAUL BERTELLI & W.K. WEISSMAN

129

NORTH ELEVATION
SCALE: 1/8" = 1'-0"

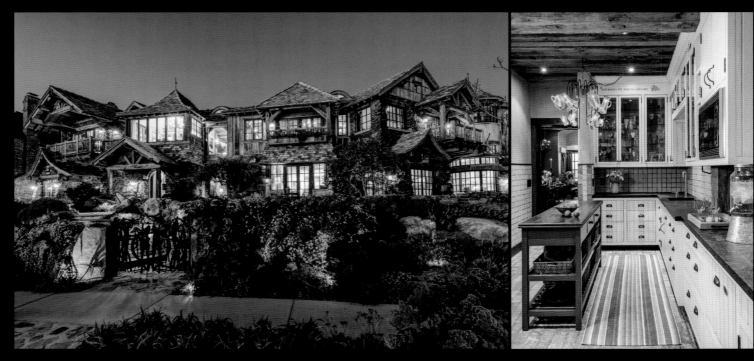

God Is Love And He That Abideth In Love Abideth In God And God In Him. 1 John 4

"SITE-SPECIFIC SCULPTURE ENTERS INTO A DIALOGUE WITH THE ARCHITECTURAL SPACE
AND THE PEDESTRIAN ARENA, CREATING A SENSE OF PLACE, IDENTITY, AND LANDMARK."

– ALBERT PALEY

143

One of JLF Design Build's recent projects is underway in Jackson Hole high atop West Gros Ventre Butte. 800-feet above the valley floor, the tranquility is disrupted by a flurry of activity at the construction site. A stack of weathered logs salvaged from the old Pipestone Hotel in Montana sits close by the construction trailer. The main building is framed-in with three central chimneys and the roof is in place. It lacks solid walls and windows and at this stage could be any half-finished house. The massive interior framework of venerable, square-cut, hand-adzed barn timbers marks it as a JLF design.

Kenny Rasmussen, the project superintendent, is the man in charge. Paul once observed that the superintendent's job is to stay focused on a single task, "building the building." A thick stack of floor plans, elevations, and detail drawings rests on a drafting table back in the trailer. All the myriad items they describe and delineate are lodged in Rasmussen's mind. It's his responsibility to make sure everything adheres to the Control Estimate. After a final check when the job is done, he'll be the last one off the site. Right now, Kenny's the go-to guy.

On a cool, early September morning, as the rising sun burns the fog off the Snake River in the valley below, several crews are busy at their tasks. On average, twenty-five plus men work here any given day. While a couple dozen elk graze on the hillside to the west, roofers perched in small maneuverable cranes install the waterproof roofing system.

145

WITHOUT THEM, JLF DESIGN BUILD'S HOUSES
WOULD BE NOTHING MORE THAN A STACK OF BLUEPRINTS.

In the yard below, skilled stonemasons carefully dress and shape lichen-covered moss rock (a form of sandstone composed of feldspar and quartz) with their sturdy mason's hammers. The masons wield them like sculptors. The stonework is remarkably accurate. "The masonry part is the hardest thing we do," Logan observed. "It takes the most experience to look at stone to recognize when it's right and when it's wrong." As evidence of this, Rasmussen points out how the masons have shaped each piece, interior and exterior, to fit around the window casements, making it seem as if the glass had been set directly into natural rock.

The project Kenny Rasmussen supervises on Gros Ventre Butte is but one of more than seventy JLF Design Build projects over the years. During that time, more than a thousand skilled builders, tradesmen, and craftspeople worked on these splendid houses. Their talent and skills are an integral part of the Process. Without them, JLF Design Build's houses would be nothing more than a stack of blueprints. The spirit of all these talented artisans imbues each structure like the medieval stonemason's mark. Along with those long-forgotten 13th Century masons, the people who built these magnificent houses might stay forever anonymous. The integrity of their work remains their only monument. ●

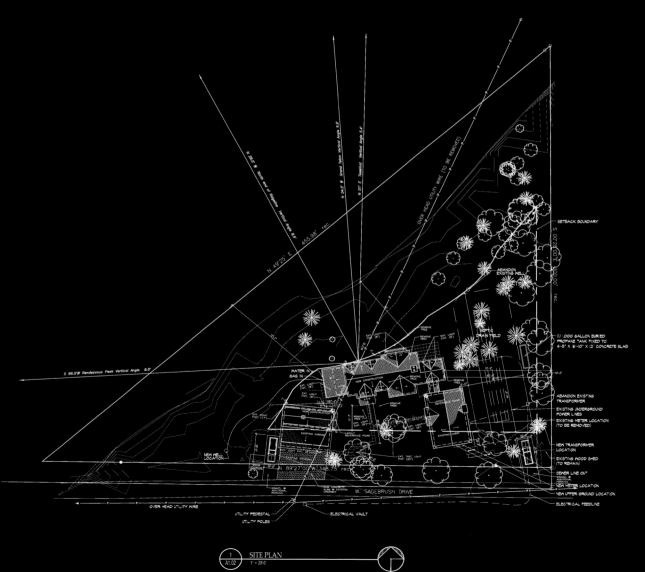

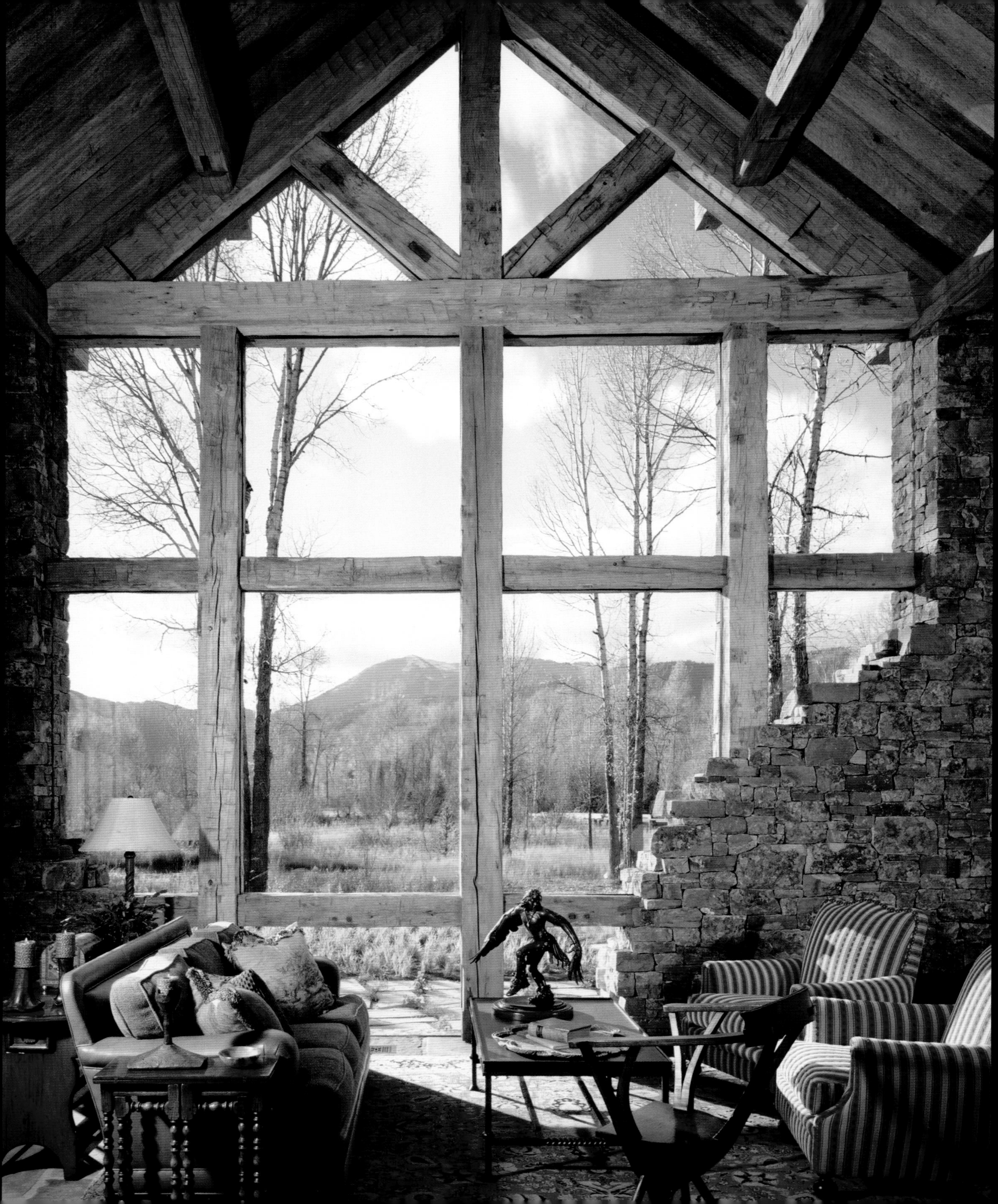

160

RUN YOUR HAND ALONG THE SCULPTED STONE OR AGAINST THE HAND-HEWN TIMBERS. CAN YOU FEEL THE POWER OF THE LABOR THAT SET THEM IN PLACE? CLOSE YOUR EYES AND HEAR THESE UNKNOWN CRAFTSPEOPLE AT WORK. THE DISTANT SOUND OF HAMMER STROKES AND THE FAINT FORGOTTEN RASP OF A CROSSCUT SAW STILL ECHO IN MEMORY. THESE STRUCTURES EMBODY THEIR ESSENCE. THEIR SPIRITS LIVE ON IN THE SPACES THEY CREATED. WE MADE THIS, THE STURDY WALLS SILENTLY PROCLAIM. OUR LIVES ARE A PART OF THIS PLACE.

WHOSE SILENT VOICES ARE THESE? TELLING THE INDIVIDUAL STORIES OF EVERYONE WHO EVER WORKED ON A JLF DESIGN BUILD SITE WOULD BE LIKE TRYING TO NAME ALL THE STARS IN THE HEAVENS. AN IMPOSSIBLE TASK. LISTEN TO THE STONES. HEAR THE DISTANT WHISPER OF THE WEATHERED WOODEN BEAMS. THOSE ANONYMOUS MEDIEVAL MASONS HAD NO ONE TO TELL THEIR STORIES. THE GRAND CATHEDRALS THEY BUILT ARE THEIR SILENT MONUMENTS. LIKEWISE, EACH ONE OF JLF DESIGN BUILD'S BEAUTIFUL HOUSES CONTAINS THE PERSONAL HISTORIES OF EVERYONE WHO LABORED TO CREATE THEM. LISTEN TO SOME OF THEIR STORIES.

Based in Victor, Idaho, the Chinker Chicks are Greta Procious and Kimberly Mills, two talented young women who have been business partners and friends for ten years. Chinking looks deceptively simple to the uninitiated but doing it right requires skill and a trained eye. Because JLF Design Build uses a lot of reclaimed timber, logs often over 100 years old, the Chinker Chicks are careful to clean away the ancient grime for better adhesion. They use a Dremel tool, grinding down through the weathered surface to find a fresh surface.

Over the years, the Chinker Chicks have worked on more JLF projects than they can remember. The connections reach back as far as The Creamery. They feel fortunate to have maintained this connection. Greta says, "Chinking looks mundane. It looks simple. It's a very Zen working environment. Our work mirrors the two of us. Looking at the final finish, you can't tell which person did it." •

CHINKING LOOKS DECEPTIVELY SIMPLE TO THE UNINITIATED BUT DOING IT RIGHT REQUIRES SKILL AND A TRAINED EYE.

DON DE CRISTO

172

Frank Horiel of Crown Creations cabinet shop in Livingston, Montana was drawn to woodworking at an early age. Frank remembers the "hand-planed shavings" in his father's shop and "a sweet smell of pine coming off the floor." The sensual aspects of his profession resonate with Horiel. "Woodworking can be very romantic," he says.

Crown Creations has a long history with JLF Design Build. "There's a mutual respect between the craftsmen and the architects and the

builders," Horiel says. "All the participants want to work together as a team to provide a product that is truly unique and of top quality to the client. The projects are pretty darn unique and challenging to the craftsman. That's part of the allure. Throughout the ages, the architect has always challenged the tradesman." Horiel praises the effort JLF makes to give their clients what they want. "They painstakingly go through the Process," he says, "because it's not always easy to find out what the client wants and then to give them that."

CABINETS BY MOUNTAIN HIGH WOODWORKS

173

Chicago-born Jim Fifles came by his love of timber frame construction early in his life. On drives into the Illinois countryside with his parents, he was fascinated to see the hundred-year-old barns dotting the landscape. "I was always drawn to it," he says. "Looking at the barns when I was a kid, I just wanted to know how they put them together." When Jack Livingood built his JLF house in Jackson Hole, Jim Fifles was hired as the timber frame subcontractor. "We went through a learning curve together on that project," Jim recalls.

While purchasing and creating an inventory of recycled beams, posts, and log stacks, Jim learned an essential truth about antique barns. "They only start to dilapidate or deteriorate when you stop using them." A working barn in good repair might last almost forever. Once it ceases to have a function, the best possible fate for an old barn is to be dismantled, its timbers recycled into another structure. This preserves the dignity of the building's long history. The labor of forgotten carpenters lives on in the distinctive adze marks and the mortises notched into the wood. Generations of farm toil remain, preserved in the timbers' weathered surfaces. The old beams celebrate the past, a far better future than consignment to a bonfire.

"We like to know what the history of the building is, where its origin was," Fifles says. Locating an entire usable log building is an asset considering the difficulties involved in trying to pair different log stacks to what the JLF design team has drawn.

Different corner notching techniques are used on cabins built with round peeled logs, but the dovetailing employed with square cut logs, all done with hand tools, is truly amazing. "The style of the notch is usually up to the original craftsman," Jim Fifles observes. "There are many different styles of corner notching. There's a saddle notch, cathedral notch, slope dovetail, and compound dovetails. It will have to do with what kind of weather conditions there are and how they shed water and keep it from getting into the logs. This old stuff, it's pretty cool stuff." •

The tools used by masons today haven't changed much from what the medieval stonecutters employed to build the cathedrals. "We still use hammers and chisels," says Pete Peterson of Jackson, Wyoming. "The only big difference is they used twenty guys to heft around a lot of this heavy stuff. We use equipment nowadays. All the actual setting and shaping of stones – what they did then is what we do now."

Pete Peterson worked on The Creamery and remembers receiving a binder of photographs from Select Stone in Gallatin Gateway, Montana, who dismantled the old building. Those pictures and JLF drawings with the primary stones numbered were the reference to how the structure looked in its original setting and how to reassemble it. "We got it back as complete as possible," Peterson recalls.

On another project, Pete is quick to observe that while all this rock might come from the same area, no two projects are alike. "I may be laying Montana moss rock from the Harlowton area on two jobs, but they very well may be a different size, a different scope. What I'm laying here is not the same thing they're laying over there. It's the same kind of rock, but it's a whole different pick and it's a whole different deal… it's the JLF team's vision." Paul and his partners have taken this to a whole new level." ●

183

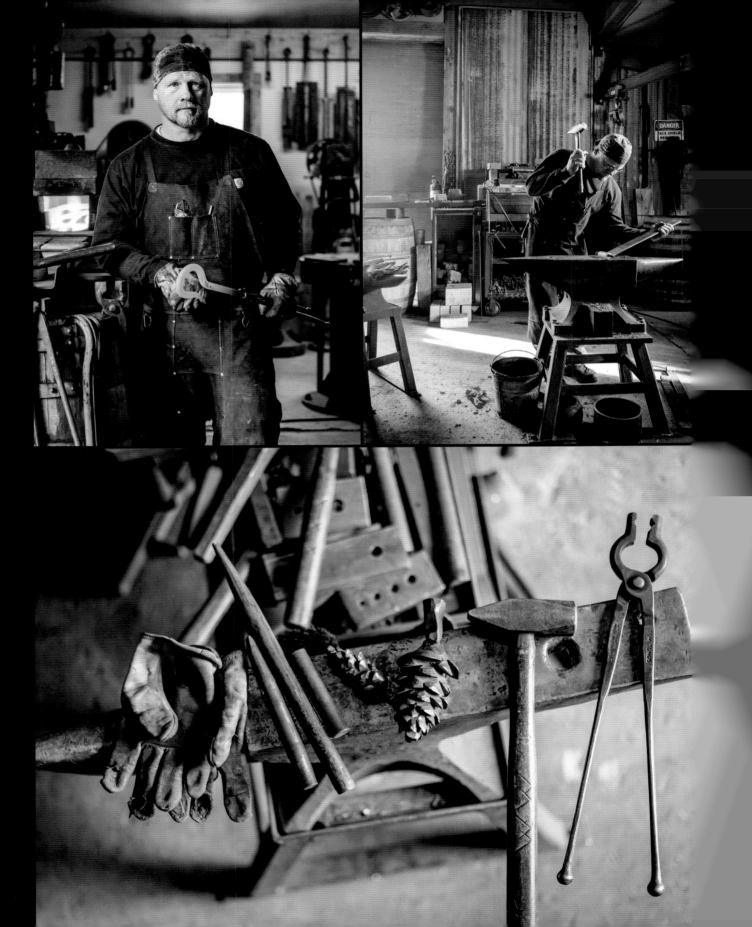

The craft of blacksmithing goes back as far into the past as the stone mason's ancient profession. Someone had to build the tools that cut and shaped the marble destined to become the Parthenon. A blacksmith's equipment and techniques haven't changed all that much over time. Metal is still heated until it is red hot and shaped with a hammer on an anvil. Forges have modernized and improved; acetylene welding, unavailable to medieval smiths, is commonplace; powered trip hammers have come into use. Even so, the heart and soul of the profession hasn't altered much since the early beginnings of the Iron Age.

Scott Espelin of Wild West Ironworks in Butte, Montana, got his start in the trade on his parent's farm in the Helena Valley. The place had its own smithy for repairing ranch equipment. "My dad would heat up a piece of steel and twist it or do something with it," Espelin recalls. "I just thought that was so interesting." After his studies at MSU College of Agriculture in Bozeman, Scott originally set up shop as a farrier in the family blacksmith shop. When he started having hip trouble, he knew his farrier days were over and feared he'd never work as a smith again.

A call came from Walt K. Weissman, an interior designer and architectural co-designer of one of the projects in this book. Walt had seen a hammered copper table supporting a cash register in a shop in Bozeman. This metalwork was not a ubiquitous clichéd product; it was special. The real challenge was finding the maker. With considerable effort and a bit of luck, Walt finally found Scott Espelin, and so began an important collaboration.

Walt needed detailed, precision work and he and Scott collaborated for almost five years. "I've never seen anyone work harder or put more heart into creating beauty," Walt commented.

"It was a process getting to know him," Scott Espelin recalled. "Walt brought into my life a vision. He breathed into me a whole new life of doing metalwork. I was just about ready to quit, give up, and go find a real job. Getting to work with him allowed me the opportunity to realize what I could do. Walt is near and dear to my heart. He's a brother to me."

"I'VE NEVER SEEN ANYONE WORK HARDER OR
PUT MORE HEART INTO CREATING BEAUTY."

Espelin spends a lot of time in the local scrap yard. "I'll be
prowling the junkyard and I'll find a piece," he says. "It might
hang around my shop for years before I find the right job to
use it on. They are seed thoughts. I get ideas from things that
other craftsmen have built years ago." Trips to the junkyard
can also be heartbreaking for Scott when he "sees things
getting loaded on train cars going to the smelter to get melted
down. That history can't be replaced." Along the way, he's
rescued several pieces of usable equipment from destruction.
His oldest power hammer dates from 1906.

Logan refers to Scott as "a steel artist," singing his praises as
he tells a story about collaboration. "I'll sit with him and say,
'Here's what I want you to do,' and he'll say, 'Okay, here's
what I'm capable of doing with the forging equipment that I
have. What if we did this? What if we moved that over there
and make the connection better?'"

"99.9 % of the time," Espelin observes, "I'm working with
steel. Anything we try to build needs to be strong and
durable. Wrought iron is weak. It's not strong. Artistically,
it looks good in a lot of things, but almost anything you can
do with iron, you can do with steel."

Espelin recalls forging hundreds of hinge barrels before he
gained the skill "to do an accurate, detailed job that would
work on rustic doors. They've got to be modern enough so
they function reliably for today's day and age." Years of labor
and exacting craftsmanship have brought Scott to the highest
level of his profession. "I've carried that over to all my work
with JLF," he observes with pride. ●

WESTERN UNION

CO-DESIGNED BY PAUL BERTELLI & W.K. WEISSMAN

Stilewood International is located in the little town of Port Coquitlam in British Columbia. Founded over twenty years ago, Stilewood is an outgrowth of a reproduction period furniture manufacturing operation begun in 1957 by Vittorio Ciccone, a European-trained architectural woodworker. The firm remains in the capable hands of Vittorio's son, Salvatore Ciccone, and specializes in producing handcrafted doors of such high quality the company slogan is "Furniture for your walls."

Stilewood has worked with JLF Design Build for more than seven years. When talking about building doors, Sal Ciccone prefers describing them as systems. "It's not just a door or a frame when you work with JLF," he says. "It's an architectural element. Each door in their design view is looked at for its place in the room as a functional design element. They take it to the level where it's not a door."

A design team from JLF visits Stilewood to have a look at a new wood shipment. Each board is stood up against the wall of the lumber storage area outside of the factory. This can involve nearly 500 feet of wall space. "It may take six boards to make one door, or one face," according to Ciccone. "JLF and our production team go through each piece of wood and identify the grouping on where that wood is actually going to reside, on which door, on which location." They examine thousands of pieces of wood. Each board is individually serial numbered. "It's like virtually bar-coded," Sal says. "It's an absolutely amazing process."

"In the twenty-five years that I have been around in the architectural door business, I can count on one hand how many architects are at that level of quality concern," Sal Ciccone says. JLF Design Build "basically does a mini architectural job on the door itself. They will design the door right down to the individual boards and their placement."

When the wood for the doors in a Jackson house was being hand-selected, John, the managing JLF architect on the project, was right there "on his hands and knees" examining the lumber on display.

"We checked off our last door," Sal recalls. "All the doors had the wood selected. Job done. We took a break, went for coffee and afterwards John says, 'Okay. Let's get back at it.'

"And my guy says, 'We've got everything.'

"And John says, 'Yeah, but there's still one more pile to go through.' A couple rows from the bottom, he found two pieces of wood that were so magnificent and very rare. He took those two pieces of wood and exchanged them – actually changed the door design on the fly. Redesigned the door from a three-vertical plank look to a two vertical plank look." The door was one of sixty installed in that house. "Absolutely very unique, very authentic," Ciccone marvels. "The process to get there is so incredible. The process to get to perfection. JLF is in all the way. They're there and they make it happen. It's a pleasure to see that within the industry in North America, we do have a firm that has that appreciation for finding excellence." ●

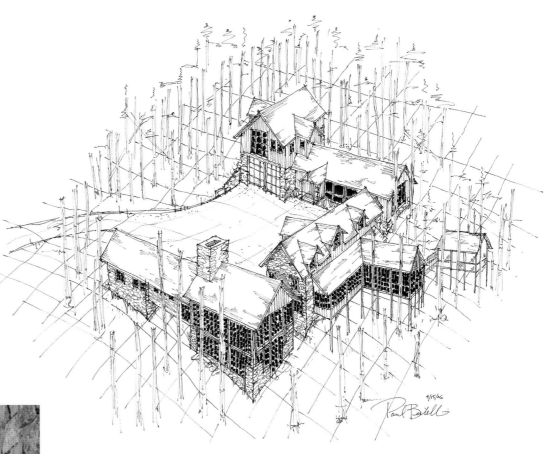

EXCELLENCE FOLLOWS COMMITMENT IS AS TRUE
AS "FORM EVER FOLLOWS FUNCTION."

— LOUIS SULLIVAN

A work of art always involves imagination springing up from some deep unknowable place even the artist finds difficult to comprehend. There is an element of faith wrapped in the enigmatic artistic process, along with trusting that hard work and talent will see a project through to its conclusion.

The pursuit of excellence is a common thread weaving through the lives of every artisan who has worked on JLF Design Build projects. Taken together, these disparate filaments form the weft of an intricate tapestry detailing the firm's essential philosophy. Integrity, empathy, harmony, passion, dedication, and collaboration are JLF Design Build's core values. The craftspeople whose work lives on within the houses they helped construct all had their talents and abilities challenged by the demanding standards of JLF Design Build. Satisfying every client remains the firm's highest priority. JLF expects everyone working on one of its projects to give the utmost of his or her talents. They set the bar as high as possible.

Working together, the management team inside JLF Design Build shares the same high expectation of excellence. The extraordinary performance standards they ask of one another are no different from what the company requires of its subcontractors. It's not a coincidence that so many of the artisans working on JLF projects say they are motivated to produce their finest work by the inspiration and integrity of the design-build philosophy. Jason has a large whiteboard mounted to the wall of his office in Jackson on which he jots inspirational messages for his team to read. In the upper right corner, Jason wrote, "The Enterprise Commitment," above a quote from Les McKowen: "When working in a team or group environment, I will place the interests of the enterprise above my personal interests." Jason uses his whiteboard like a coach diagramming plays, encouraging the team with inspirational quotes.

The emphasis is always on group endeavor. Teamwork provides the cornerstone of JLF Design Build's value list that celebrates hard work, diligence, personal responsibility, dependability, commitment, and a host of other virtues all very useful for an individual but absolutely indispensable for any collective enterprise. When JLF surveyed their employees about values, their enthusiastic replies included, "Building relationships through trust," "Pride in our work and dedication to quality," and "Joy we give to clients through our efforts." This is an earnest expression of team spirit devoted to serving the client. One employee wrote that the firm's purpose was "to enable people to live beautiful lives." Paul observes that when doing something so complex as designing and building a house, there should be a single source of responsibility. The collaboration between an architectural firm and a construction company is at the heart of the Process and provides the client with the best both have to offer, "leadership."

Dunlop once wrote a John Hamm quote on his whiteboard: "Content is dead – long live storytelling." He followed it with another quote from Seth Godin: "Either you're going to tell stories that spread, or you're going to become irrelevant." The JLF Design Build story has spread not only across the physical landscape with each new distinctive house it creates, but the images of its remarkable structures also populate the interior landscape of the imagination. Every project tells its own story. Clients, artisans, and designers all have a tale to tell. Taken together, they become part of a larger narrative.

The story of JLF Design Build is not just a history of two companies working in harmony. It is a complex drama involving hundreds of individuals: architects, designers, draftsmen, supervisors, engineers, carpenters, stone masons, electricians, chinkers, everyone who swings a hammer or works with AutoCAD or pours concrete, each person working at

SHOW UP EVERYDAY, KEEP YOUR HEAD DOWN, LOVE WHAT YOU DO, AND THE PEOPLE YOU DO IT WITH, AND YOU CAN ACCOMPLISH EXTRAORDINARY THINGS.

216

the top of his ability at the service of the client, all of them joining in a greater purpose. Over time, they all become true partners in the project. Brothers connected by hard work.

"Our common thread is that we all have a passion and honesty about the work," Paul observes. "There's some synergistic thing where everyone's craft all comes together to be something greater than the sum of its parts." This common bond is the epitome of everything JLF Design Build stands for in their quest for perfection.

Designing and building houses that are works of art is more than a job. It is a fraternity, a calling to strive for the best, a brotherhood of skilled and talented individuals all committed in their hearts and minds, each giving the utmost of his and her abilities to the project, a "guild" of our time.

Architecture must be seen up close and in person to appreciate the artistry involved in its creation. It is five-dimensional art when you include "light and time." The inside of any building is just as important as the outside. All the owners of JLF Design Build houses know this first hand. They have the privilege of living in works of art. Ownership is transitory. Many decades into the future, other families will occupy these magnificent houses. They've been built to last a very long time. Only art endures. The work of JLF Design Build will remain long after the passing of everyone reading these words. It will inspire and delight unborn generations still to come. Like the silent beauty of the medieval cathedrals, these magnificent works are a testament to the enduring creative spirit of mankind. •

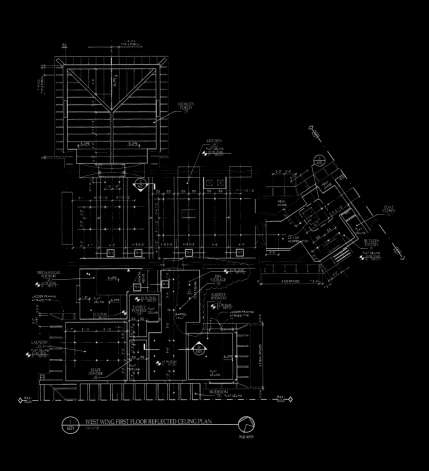

WEST WING FIRST FLOOR REFLECTED CEILING PLAN

NORTH ELEVATION
1/8" = 1'-0"

"ONE DAY, THIRTY YEARS LATER, YOU LOOK BACK AT
THE BODY OF WORK AND YOU THINK, WE DID ALL THAT?"

BIOGRAPHIES

THE WORK OF ART

PAUL BERTELLI + JLF & ASSOCIATES

Paul Bertelli is the Senior Design Principal and President of JLF & Associates. Beginning in 1979, Paul and Jon Foote worked together for 21 years before Paul purchased the firm with partners Tammy Hauer and Logan Leachman. Paul studied architecture at Boston Architectural Center in Boston, Massachusetts and at Montana State University in Bozeman, Montana. He holds a Bachelor of Arts degree in Environmental Design and a Master of Architecture. Paul is currently a board member of the Montana State University School of Architecture Advisory Council, a founding board member and current advisory board member of the Yellowstone Business Partnership, a current advisory board member of the Yellowstone Park Foundation, and a past trustee of the Museum of the Rockies. Paul is a much sought-after designer who has created some of the most unique houses in the country.

When Paul is not practicing architecture, he enjoys fly fishing in pristine, remote waters. He is an avid skier and frequents the steep slopes at Bridger Bowl and Big Sky. A foodie at heart, he enjoys both cooking and sampling gourmet food and wine. One can also see him around Bozeman on the hiking trail with his stepdaughter Amelie, and wife Jillian.

TAMMY HAUER + JLF & ASSOCIATES

Tammy, Principal and CFO, is an assiduous financial and human resources manager. She is responsible for managing all aspects of internal controls as well as exploring growth opportunities for the firm and its employees. Financial planning and analysis, budget development and management, accounting operations, staff management, cash forecasts, internal audits, and pension plan management are a small list of her various areas of expertise. Tammy became an owner of JLF & Associates in 2000. Since that ownership transition, the firm has an established record of strong financial success.

Prior to her venture into the architectural world, Tammy began her financial career path in the 1980's as Deputy Treasurer for Park County. She moved from the government sector to a more creative venue working with world renowned artist Russell Chatham as his business manager. After hearing of her strong business savvy, Jonathan Foote asked her to join his team in 1987. Tammy has furthered her education by earning her Project Management Certification from the University of Phoenix.

Tammy shares her life with her husband, Monte, and their four children. She has a strong passion for music and entertaining. You can find her regularly singing and playing her acoustic guitar at several Montana businesses and events.

LOGAN LEACHMAN + JLF & ASSOCIATES

Logan began his career in 1992 under firm leadership of Jonathan L. Foote. In 2000, upon Jonathan's retirement, Logan joined Paul and Tammy as partners and founding members of what is now referred to as JLF & Associates, Inc. Logan has been a driving force behind many of the firm's most successful projects. Logan was instrumental in forming many of the methods JLF Design Build practices today, a process he continues to champion and refine. He is responsible for designs, project management, company policy, and corporate analytics.

Logan studied architecture at Western Kentucky University in the mid 1980's where he met his wife Jamie. They moved west in 1990 and started a family. All three of his children were raised in Montana where they all enjoy an active, outdoor lifestyle. Logan enjoys traveling to new worldly destinations usually with his bike in tow, skiing in the beautiful mountains of Montana, and gardening. He is pleased that his daughter, Morgan, chose to study architecture while interning at the firm and carry on his passion for beautiful, responsible design.

ASHLEY SULLIVAN + JLF & ASSOCIATES

JOHN M. LAUMAN + JLF & ASSOCIATES

JAKE SCOTT + JLF & ASSOCIATES

Ashley is a design Principal and registered architect at JLF & Associates. She studied and earned her Bachelor of Architecture at Auburn University. Ashley's design-build background began on the Hay Bale House during the first year of Rural Studio (1994) under "Sambo" Mockbee. Here she developed her respect for clients' needs, place-based design, and craft. She continues to expand her knowledge as she collaborates with her design-build partners, craftsmen, and artists. Ashley grew up in Nashville, Tennessee and has merged her Southern lady charm with a relaxed Mountain West lifestyle. Her background, cultural experiences, and desire to learn have given her a unique perspective on life.

Ashley renews her inspiration through her connection with nature and culture. She can often be spotted rafting the Yellowstone River or taking a few turns on the slopes of Bridger Bowl or Big Sky. She also enjoys backpacking and cross country skiing in the silence of the forests trails in the Absaroka-Beartooth Mountain Ranges. She loves to travel and expand her cultural mindset. Her friends and family know her best for enjoying a glass of wine while engaging in wonderful conversation, laughter, and inspirational thoughts.

Like the backstory that plays behind the opening title credits of a typical 80's movie, John was raised in a small mining/farming community in southeast Idaho, studied architecture at Montana State University and began his career in Jackson, Wyoming. After two short years and a chance meeting with some JLF employees, he began working for JLF & Associates in July of 1997. Over the years, he has grown from a green intern to Partner, helping expand the company's resume of diverse projects and satisfied clients. He always endeavors to far surpass the client's expectations. He is excited to help mold the future of the company and intends to ensure that the legacy of JLF endures. John is a devoted husband, loving father of two daughters, and obsessive fly-fisherman of the incredible waters of Montana and the world.

Jake began working with JLF & Associates in 1999 as an intern, rising through the ranks to become a Partner. Jake has managed projects ranging from small guest houses to ranches and resort facilities. He works closely with clients and team members from programming through construction to make every project successful. Before starting at JLF, Jake moved from Vermont to Bozeman where he graduated with a Master of Architecture from Montana State University. He is an architect, a LEED Accredited Professional and a member of the U.S. Green Building Council (USGBC). He is currently serving as the board president of the Bozeman Film Festival. Jake and his wife, Stacey, enjoy camping in the beautiful Montana summers. In the winter they enjoy traveling to more distant locations.

BIOGRAPHIES
THE WORK OF ART

JACK LIVINGOOD + BIG-D SIGNATURE

Jack has been blessed with a lifelong passion for collaborative and principal based design and construction. A third generation builder and perpetual student of the construction industry, Jack followed his father into the family business in 1978 and became President in 1988. As Big-D's CEO he has dedicated his life's work to creating an environment for outstanding careers and world-class customer service. Along the way, he has grown the Big-D family of companies into one of the most respected, innovative, and sought after companies in the business. He lives in Jackson Hole, Wyoming with his wife Jodi and son Jackson.

SCOTT DANSIE + BIG-D SIGNATURE

Scott, no doubt, grew up with "Lincoln Logs" and building blocks. Construction is wired into his genetic code. As a young man, he worked as a construction laborer, pipe layer, heavy equipment operator, grade checker, and carpenter. Since graduating from BYU in Construction Management, his entire professional life has been spent in the construction industry, with particular emphasis on preconstruction services and premier resort area construction. Scott started at Signature as the Operations Manager before moving into the role of President, in charge of the company's overall daily operations. He has been a driving force at Big-D Signature from its inception and instrumental in developing many of the best practices and processes that set Big-D Signature apart. Scott and his wife have five children and live near Park City, Utah. His outdoor pursuits include skiing, hiking, cycling, and off-road motorcycling.

LAYNE THOMPSON + BIG-D SIGNATURE

Layne, Vice President, began working at Big-D Signature in 2005, rounding out the team's vision for high quality estimating, scheduling, and construction management processes. In his early years working with JLF, he had the opportunity to contribute directly on some of JLF Design Build's most recognized projects including the Creamery, Twin Creeks, and Lazy J Ranch. Layne's expertise helped build Signature into one of the region's finest high-end residential construction companies, utilizing sophisticated budgeting, estimating, and scheduling to provide exceptional service, accuracy, and attention to detail. Layne is a native of Jackson, Wyoming and enjoys spending time in the outdoors with his wife and three children.

JASON DUNLOP + BIG-D SIGNATURE

Jason has been involved in a number of aspects of the
construction industry, beginning his career in the field as a
carpenter, being promoted to project engineer, project manager,
and eventually transitioning into business development.
As Vice President, he is an invaluable member of the
Signature management team. His responsibilities include
field operations, safety, training, and business development.
He served as Chair of the U.S. Green Building Council
(USGBC) in Wyoming and is currently serving as the National
Membership Seat of the USGBC Chapter Steering Committee.
He is the only LEED AP for Homes in Wyoming. Jason also
volunteers his time to help various other non-profit
organizations including Team Jackson Hole, Teton Adaptive
Sports, National Ability Center, and Habitat for Humanity in
both Jackson, Wyoming and Park City, Utah. Jason lives
in Jackson Hole, with his wife and three kids. He is an avid cyclist,
loves backcountry skiing, and is a self-proclaimed tech geek.

THE JLF DESIGN - BUILD PROCESS

THE WORK OF ART

PROCESS SUMMARY:
Planning and Programming.
Working Program and Budget.
Preliminary Design – "concept diagrams."
Schematic Design and Budget Revisions.
Design Development.
Design Development Value Engineering and Budget Revisions.
Construction Documents.
Construction Documents Cost Control and Value Engineering.
Bid and Negotiation.
Construction Administration.
Aftercare and Warranty.

PLANNING AND PROGRAMMING:
(owner, construction management, architect, project architect)
Establish philosophy, family goals, and expectations. "Why are we doing this? What is our purpose."
Review owner's (family's) inspirational materials and ideas.
Review general spatial requirements.
Review material likes and dislikes, inspirations, and potential.
Enumerate/articulate specific rooms and their sizes. List alternative sizes.
Incorporate gross spatial requirements: walls, partitions, fireplaces, etc.
Include unglamorous spatial requirements: mechanical rooms, etc.
Program exterior spaces: patios, decks, porches, paved areas, etc.
Itemize utilities and infrastructure: trenching, power, water, septic, driveways, generators, etc.
Itemize and identify consultant disciplines required.
Itemize landscaping and interior design needs.
Review schedule expectations.
Review architectural contract and submit drafts for discussion and subsequent signature.
Review design-build contract types and submit drafts for disclosure.
Owner communicates budget expectations to architect or owner requests architect to prepare a working budget range based on program requirements.

WORKING PROGRAM AND BUDGET:
Given the above information, two project "scopes" – consisting of room and area sizes in square feet – are developed. To establish a range of costs (financial "goal posts"), two preliminary square foot costs (one higher, one lower) are applied to the square foot areas. Line items for utilities, infrastructure, consultants, architecture, and miscellaneous costs (landscaping, interior design) are budgeted. Costs are based on team input, response to site conditions, owner's preliminary material choices, up to date current market conditions, and schedule demands.
Submit preliminary program and budget for review.
Team response to owner's questions, alternatives, additions, deletions.
Rework and resubmit program and budget.
Review insurance requirements.
Repeat as required.

Obtain owner's approval of program and budget.
(During this programming phase, we are gathering pertinent design technical data, topo survey, geotech information, sight lines to key landscape elements, preliminary review with ARC, etc.)

PRELIMINARY DESIGN – CONCEPT DIAGRAMS:
Establish spatial relationships of building components.
Establish spatial relationships of building to site including exterior spaces.
Produce graphic, scaled bubble diagrams of these concepts.
Present and review with owner and team.
Approve preliminary concepts.
Revise program and budget per concept if differs from preliminary program and budget.
Develop preliminary critical path schedule design through commissioning.
Owner approval of preliminary concept and budget revisions.
Discuss interior design delivery methods.

SCHEMATIC DESIGN AND BUDGET REVISIONS:
Produce schematic site plan (usually hand drawn).
Produce schematic floor plans (hand drawn).
Produce schematic elevations (hand drawn).
Produce necessary sections or details to better illustrate the design concepts.
Provide preliminary landscape and hardscape design.
Revise program.
Revise the budget using the more detailed process of "quantity cost" estimating utilizing the SD drawings to accurately measure the building and quantify materials.
Present schematic design and revised quantity cost estimate to owner.
Review and develop ideas and design with owner (spatial and material).
Review design and construction schedule.
Revise schematic as required.
Obtain owner approval of schematic design and schematic design budget.
Present and review with appropriate architectural review committees (ARC).
Develop critical path schedule for architect deliverables, owner decisions, and construction.
Finalize design-build contract type and questions.

DESIGN DEVELOPMENT:
Convert all schematic design drawings to CAD/Revit.
Build model if required (owner or ARC) (budget as required) (digital, wood, pressboard).
Develop wall assemblies and structural systems.
Develop landscape and hardscape.
Assemble and review exterior materials, develop mockups as required (stone walls, timbers, roofing, window type, etc.).
Obtain owner approval.
Develop "all" interior finishes, concepts and materials, walls, ceilings, floors, tile, cabinetry, faucets, fittings, fixtures, appliances, hardware, lighting, sample boards, and cut sheets.
Present to owner for approval and revisions.
Develop unique finishes, waxes, stains, paint techniques.

Present CAD/Revit drawing developments to owner: exact room dimensions, window compositions, volumes, elevations, sections, details, etc.
Develop preliminary furniture plan.
ARC review as required.

235

DESIGN DEVELOPMENT VALUE ENGINEERING AND BUDGET REVISIONS:
Engage all consultant disciplines and potential subcontractors to develop, resolve system conflicts, and typology.
Disseminate preliminary drawings to subcontractors and consultants.
Obtain subcontractor feedback on choice of assembly systems and materials and cost controls.
Revise design development budget (team and subcontractor input).
Present alternative materials, products, equipment, and designs for cost control and value engineering.
Document owner choices and incorporate into construction documents.
Develop scope of work and R.F.P. for interior design consultant.
Revise design development budget for owner approval.
Revise schedule.
Repeat as required.
Obtain owner approval of design development choices and budget.

CONSTRUCTION DOCUMENTS:
Develop all details and schedules.
Develop bid documents.
Review mechanical/electrical/lighting systems and design with owner.
Revise as required.
Revise and review landscape design (prebid).
Complete specifications and construction documents.
Owner review of plans to date.
Develop undecided finishes and architectural elements (based on critical path needs of construction management team).
Review interior design R.F.P.'s and selections.

CONSTRUCTION DOCUMENTS COST CONTROL AND VALUE ENGINEERING:
Incorporate value engineering elements and subcontractor feedback into construction documents.
Start subcontractor vetting process (construction team, architect, consultants).
Distribute preliminary sets to subs for pre-bid meetings.
Review alternatives and potential savings with owner.
Incorporate revisions and value engineering suggestions into construction bid sets.
Review construction contract methods and details.

BID AND NEGOTIATION:
Disseminate bid sets to subcontractors, two or three qualified subs per trade (construction management, project architect).

Conduct bid meetings and document review.
Clarify and revise drawings as required.
Review bid submittals with owner and team.
Discuss and review missing elements; quantify and qualify bids.
Recommend and assemble final bids, budgets, and schedules.
Identify allowances and undecided elements; quantify and establish budgets.
Produce "control estimate," revise and approve as required.
Review and confirm builder's risk insurance requirements.
Owner approval and signature of contract and control estimate.
Owner provides notice to proceed.

CONSTRUCTION ADMINISTRATION:
Revise and "cost load" the schedule.
Review potential use of owner accessible construction control software.
Weekly consultants/biweekly construction meetings.
Respond and clarify Requests for Information (RFI), Requests for Proposal (RFP), Architect's Supplemental Instructions (ASI), etc.
Conduct and lead monthly budget meetings (owner, construction management team, architect).
Coincide with "application for payment" review and approval.
Continue mockups, finishes, and materials.
Review site conditions and subcontractor aesthetic compliance (daily, weekly, or monthly as required).
Finalize critical path undecided and interiors package with all relevant team members.
Revise and review interior design submittals.
Photograph/document miscellaneous details.
Submit progress reports and photos, team process and participation.
Solve anomalies and conflicts.
Administer and lead punch list process.
Review closeout documents, owner's manuals, and building commissioning.
Attend the team barbeque and closeout party.

AFTERCARE AND WARRANTY:
Conduct quality assurance and building performance review at one year anniversary of completion (construction management team, architect, owner, consultants as required).
Continued owner feedback: suggestions, additions, changes, and follow-up.
Provide both design and construction input as needs change and modifications to project are desired.
Follow an abbreviated version of the process above whenever a modification is desired by the owner (family), so they can make informed decisions relative to cost, schedule, and aesthetics.
Extended service care and warranty are available.

ACKNOWLEDGEMENTS

THE WORK OF ART

FIRST AND FOREMOST, WE ARE ETERNALLY GRATEFUL TO ALL OUR CLIENTS – NOT JUST THOSE FEATURED HERE. WITHOUT THEM, WE WOULD NOT HAVE HAD THE OPPORTUNITY OR THE GOOD FORTUNE TO CREATE THESE BUILDINGS. THE HOUSES ARE YOURS, NOT OURS. WE HOPE THEY FOREVER BRING AS MUCH JOY TO YOU AS THEY BROUGHT TO US CREATING THEM.

MANY THANKS TO GORDON GOFF AND RYAN BURESH AT ORO FOR THEIR ENCOURAGEMENT AND PATIENCE.

SPECIAL THANKS TO DAN BRYANT FOR YOUR VISION AND FOR TAKING ON SOMETHING NEW, LIKE A RAINBOW TO A FLY; A CHALLENGE YOU HAVE RISEN TO WITH STRENGTH AND STYLE. THANK YOU ALSO TO DESIGNERS, DANNY LOUTEN AND ANN ABBOTT WHO WORK WITH YOU AT "MAKE."

THANKS K.C. FOR INTRODUCING US TO DAN. SIMM'S WADERS ARE THE BEST IN THE WORLD!

TO AUDREY HALL, YOU AND YOUR CAMERA'S EYE BROUGHT LIFE AND LIGHT TO OUR WORK. YOU HAVE BEEN A PART OF OUR FAMILY SINCE YOUR HAIR GOT CAUGHT IN THE ELECTRIC ERASER; WE WILL NEVER LET YOU GO! THANKS TODD FOR SHARING HER WITH US.

THANK YOU SO MUCH GATZ; YOU ARE OUR VOICE. IT'S JUST LIKE WRITING A SCREENPLAY, BUT NOT LIKE AN 880 PAGE BIOGRAPHY OF RICHARD BRAUTIGAN!

TO DAVID QUAMMEN, YOU ARE A GIFT TO OUR COMMUNITY, A HUMORIST WITH SERIOUS STUFF, AND A DEAR FRIEND.

WE AND ALL OF OUR CLIENTS WHO HAVE WORN A PATH IN THEIR FLOORS WOULD LIKE TO ACKNOWLEDGE THE HOSPITALITY AND GRACIOUSNESS OF CAROL AND PETER COXHEAD.

TO THE INTERIOR DESIGNERS WHO COMPLETE US AND GIVE OUR WORK A SENSE OF COMFORT.

THANKS TO DICK STORBO; YOU ARE NOT HERE NOW, BUT YOU HELPED US TAKE THAT RISK IN THE BEGINNING.

TO JIM VERDONE FOR GROUNDING US AND OUR BUILDINGS IN THE EARTH.

THANK YOU TO ALL THE PHOTOGRAPHERS (NOT ALL OF YOU ARE IN THIS BOOK) WHO OVER THE YEARS HAVE SHOT OUR PROJECTS. YOUR PHOTOS ARE PRECIOUS AND ESSENTIAL. VERY FEW PEOPLE GET TO PHYSICALLY SET FOOT INSIDE THESE HOUSES, MOSTLY OUT OF RESPECT FOR OUR CLIENTS' PRIVACY. IT'S BECAUSE OF YOU THAT MANY MORE PEOPLE WILL GET TO EXPERIENCE OUR WORK.

TO BECKY FOR THE LATE HOURS AND LOST LUNCHES.

TO JASON AND LARA AT BIG-D FOR THEIR INVALUABLE ASSISTANCE.

TO WALT, ED, BOB, AND ROBERTA FOR THEIR FRIENDSHIP, LOVE, AND SUPPORT.

THANK YOU TO OUR FAMILIES WHO NURTURE US: JILLIAN, MONTE, JAMIE, KRISTIN, STACEY, JODI, CAROL, KELLY, AND LAURA. THIS IS MODEST RECOMPENSE FOR ALL THE TIME WE SPEND AWAY FROM THOSE WE LOVE THE MOST.

TO ALL OF YOU AT BIG-D, JLF, AND OSM – IT TAKES AN EXTRAORDINARY TEAM OF PEOPLE TO ACCOMPLISH THIS WORK; YOU ARE THEM. IT IS BECAUSE WE TRUST EACH OTHER THAT SO FEW CAN ACHIEVE SO MUCH. EVERYONE OF YOU HAS CONTRIBUTED TO THE SUCCESS AND BEAUTY OF THIS WORK. IT IS HECTIC AROUND HERE ALL THE TIME. IT IS NOT OFTEN WE STOP AND THANK YOU FOR YOUR COMMITMENT AND HARD WORK. WE SAY IT HERE AS LOUD AS WE CAN: WE ARE PROUD OF YOU ALL! THANK YOU.

IN MEMORY OF SARAH MORGAN

INDEX

INDEX

THE WORK OF ART

PHOTOGRAPHER AUDREY HALL

PHOTOGRAPHER AUDREY HALL

PHOTOGRAPHER AUDREY HALL

PHOTOGRAPHER AUDREY HALL

PHOTOGRAPHER AUDREY HALL

PHOTOGRAPHER AUDREY HALL
INTERIOR DESIGN JLF

PHOTOGRAPHER AUDREY HALL
INTERIOR DESIGN LAURA WHITE

PHOTOGRAPHER AUDREY HALL

PHOTOGRAPHER AUDREY HALL
INTERIOR DESIGN TAYLOE PIGGOTT

PHOTOGRAPHER AUDREY HALL
INTERIOR FURNISHINGS INTERIOR ENVIRONMENTS, INC.
INTERIOR FINISHES JLF, MAKE

PHOTOGRAPHER AUDREY HALL

PHOTOGRAPHER AUDREY HALL

INDEX
THE WORK OF ART

100   **101**

PHOTOGRAPHER AUDREY HALL
INTERIOR DESIGN HENRY SMEDLEY AND KATHY CHOW

102   **103**

PHOTOGRAPHER AUDREY HALL

104   **105**

PHOTOGRAPHER AUDREY HALL
INTERIOR FURNISHINGS ASSOCIATES III INTERIOR DESIGN
INTERIOR FINISHES JLF

112   **113**

PHOTOGRAPHER AUDREY HALL
KITCHEN CABINETRY JLF, WILD WEST IRON WORKS, INC., AND SKIDMORE, INC.

114   **115**

PHOTOGRAPHER AUDREY HALL
INTERIOR DESIGN ARNELL KASE AND HEATHER MADDEN DESIGN
KITCHEN CABINETRY JLF, WILD WEST IRON WORKS, INC., AND SKIDMORE, INC.

116   **117**

PHOTOGRAPHER AUDREY HALL
INTERIOR DESIGN ARNELL KASE AND HEATHER MADDEN DESIGN
KITCHEN CABINETRY JLF, WILD WEST IRON WORKS, INC., AND SKIDMORE, INC.

124   **125**

PHOTOGRAPHER AUDREY HALL
INTERIOR DESIGN W.K. WEISSMAN

126   **127**

PHOTOGRAPHER AUDREY HALL
BUILDER (LEFT TO RIGHT) OSM, CAPSTONE CONSTRUCTION, JLF DESIGN-BUILD
INTERIOR DESIGN ALESSANDRA BRANCA (LIVING ROOM)

128   **129**

PHOTOGRAPHER AUDREY HALL

136   **137**

PHOTOGRAPHER AUDREY HALL
INTERIOR DESIGN TLM INTERIOR DESIGNERS
SCULPTOR ALBERT PALEY (LIGHT FIXTURE + FIREPLACE SCREEN)

138   **139**

PHOTOGRAPHER AUDREY HALL
INTERIOR DESIGN TLM INTERIOR DESIGNERS

140   **141**

PHOTOGRAPHER AUDREY HALL
LANDSCAPE KRISTIANSEN ASSOCIATES
LANDSCAPE DESIGN VLA, INC.

106 107

PHOTOGRAPHER AUDREY HALL

108 109

PHOTOGRAPHER AUDREY HALL
INTERIOR DESIGN HILARY HEMINWAY INTERIORS

110 111

PHOTOGRAPHER AUDREY HALL
INTERIOR DESIGN ARNELL KASE AND HEATHER MADDEN DESIGN

118 119

120 121

PHOTOGRAPHER AUDREY HALL
INTERIOR DESIGN W.K. WEISSMAN

122 123

PHOTOGRAPHER AUDREY HALL
INTERIOR DESIGN W.K. WEISSMAN

130 131

PHOTOGRAPHER AUDREY HALL
INTERIOR DESIGN R. HIGGINS INTERIORS
CABINETRY DESIGN JLF

132 133

PHOTOGRAPHER AUDREY HALL
INTERIOR DESIGN R. HIGGINS INTERIORS

134 135

PHOTOGRAPHER AUDREY HALL

142 143

PHOTOGRAPHERS AUDREY HALL, WILLIAM DUBOIS (CENTER)
INTERIOR DESIGN TLM INTERIOR DESIGNERS
SCULPTOR ALBERT PALEY

144 145

PHOTOGRAPHER AUDREY HALL

146 147

PHOTOGRAPHER AUDREY HALL

INDEX
THE WORK OF ART

154 155

PHOTOGRAPHER AUDREY HALL
INTERIOR DESIGN ED

156 157

PHOTOGRAPHERS (LEFT + BOTTOM RIGHT) LOGAN LEACHMAN, AUDREY HALL
INTERIOR DESIGN ED

158 159

PHOTOGRAPHERS (LEFT TO RIGHT) ©PAUL WARCHOL, PVB
BUILDER OSM
INTERIOR DESIGN HILARY HEMINWAY INTERIORS

166 167

PHOTOGRAPHER AUDREY HALL

168 169

PHOTOGRAPHER AUDREY HALL
INTERIOR DESIGN TAYLOE PIGGOTT

170 171

PHOTOGRAPHER AUDREY HALL

247

178 179

PHOTOGRAPHER AUDREY HALL

180 181

PHOTOGRAPHER AUDREY HALL
INTERIOR DESIGN TAYLOE PIGGOTT

182 183

PHOTOGRAPHER AUDREY HALL

190 191

PHOTOGRAPHER AUDREY HALL

192 193

PHOTOGRAPHERS (LEFT TO RIGHT) LOGAN LEACHMAN, AUDREY HALL

194 195

PHOTOGRAPHER AUDREY HALL

INDEX
THE WORK OF ART

PHOTOGRAPHER AUDREY HALL
INTERIOR DESIGN MATTHEW CARTER INTERIORS

PHOTOGRAPHERS PVB, ©JLF & ASSOCIATES, INC.
BUILDERS OSM (LEFT + RIGHT) STEVE SIMPSON / LOG DOGS (CENTER)

PHOTOGRAPHER AUDREY HALL
BUILDER OSM
INTERIOR DESIGN CATHERINE LANE INTERIORS

PHOTOGRAPHER AUDREY HALL

PHOTOGRAPHERS AUDREY HALL, LOGAN LEACHMAN (BOTTOM RIGHT)

PHOTOGRAPHER AUDREY HALL
BUILDER OSM

PHOTOGRAPHERS (LEFT TO RIGHT) AUDREY HALL, LOGAN LEACHMAN

PHOTOGRAPHER AUDREY HALL

PHOTOGRAPHER AUDREY HALL

JLF & ASSOCIATES' APPROACH TO PHILANTHROPY IS AS THOUGHTFUL, COMPLEX, AND DEDICATED TO BEAUTY AS THEIR ARCHITECTURAL WORK. THEIR GOAL IS TO ALLOW PHILANTHROPIC INSPIRATION TO BECOME REALITY. THEY BELIEVE THEIR BUSINESS IS A PROCESS, NOT A PRODUCT, AND THEIR GIVING IS MOTIVATED BY THE SAME UNDERSTANDING. BOTH PARTNERS AND STAFF, WHO MAKE UP THE JFA CHARITABLE FUND GIFTING COMMITTEE, PARTICIPATE IN THE PHILANTHROPIC DECISION-MAKING PROCESS. THE PARTNERS OF JLF & ASSOCIATES BELIEVE THEY ARE LUCKY TO DO WHAT THEY DO AND GIVING BACK ONLY ENRICHES THE EXPERIENCE. "WE ARE INTERESTED IN BECOMING MORE CONNECTED, IN BECOMING BETTER DESIGNERS, BETTER BUSINESSPEOPLE, BETTER CITIZENS, AND IN CONTRIBUTING TO OUR COLLECTIVE QUALITY OF LIFE."

THE JFA CHARITABLE FUND IS DEDICATED TO HELPING FOSTER INNOVATIVE PROGRAMS, INITIATIVES, AND IDEAS WHICH ENHANCE THE COMMUNITY AND THE REGION SURROUNDING US. THE GEOGRAPHICAL INTERESTS OF THE FUND ARE DIRECTLY RELATED TO THE LOVE AND DEDICATION THE OWNERS AND EMPLOYEES OF JLF & ASSOCIATES FEEL FOR THIS UNIQUE PLACE. THE JFA CHARITABLE FUND IS DEDICATED TO SUPPORTING ORGANIZATIONS THAT PROMOTE AWARENESS IN AREAS OF INTEREST INCLUDING EDUCATION, ENVIRONMENT, CONSERVATION, QUALITY OF LIFE, STEWARDSHIP, RESPONSIBLE GROWTH, AND SUSTAINABLE COMMUNITIES.

THE JFA CHARITABLE FUND RECOGNIZES THE EXTRAORDINARY NEEDS OF OUR COMMUNITY. WE BELIEVE IN THE POWER AND SYNERGISTIC NATURE OF GIVING. WE HOPE TO NURTURE, BY EXAMPLE, THE JOY AND RESPONSIBILITY OF THIS ENDEAVOR.